NEWBORN
NE$T EGG

The 1-HOUR Formula Enabling New Parents
to Turn Pocket Change into a Million-Dollar
'Safety Nest' for Their Children

DEPENDANT
PUBLISHING

Copyright © 2024 by R. Fast

This book is published by Dependant Publishing, a subsidiary of R. Fast Wealth Strategies.

The business address is:

24266 61 Ave. Langley BC, Canada V2Y 2G2

Please visit the associated websites for more information: www.dependantpublishing.com, www.fastwealth.com, and www.newbornnestegg.com

Newborn Nest Egg: The 1-HOUR formula Enabling New Parents to Turn Pocket Change into a Million-Dollar 'Safety Nest' for their Children

Includes Index:

ISBN 978-1-0689606-0-4 (Paperback)

ISBN 978-1-0689606-1-1 (eBook)

CONTENTS

NEWBORN NE$T EGG

"Someone's sitting in the shade
today because someone planted
a tree a long time ago."

– Warren Buffett –

CHAPTER 1

THE SAFETY NEST

Inspiration

How do poultry farmers get their hens to lay more eggs? Do they play classical music, let the birds run free outside all day, precisely regulate barn temperature, or maybe feed them a special diet?

This was the exact question poultry farmers set out to answer a few hundred years ago. If they could get the same number of hens to produce more eggs, that would mean more income and higher profits. What some of them discovered was that if they placed an artificial egg in each nest, the hens would lay more eggs. This is where the term "nest egg" comes from. What a great way to multiply wealth!

Today, the term nest egg has morphed into a generic description for a sizable sum of money, typically set aside for retirement. Most people start thinking about saving for retirement in their 30s, with the hopes that they can accumulate enough to stop working by about age 65. This book will challenge that way of thinking in two fundamental ways: 1) you shouldn't wait till your 30s or later to start making arrangements for retirement, and 2) retirement is not an age but a lifelong system of financial freedom.

It is no secret that life is getting more expensive. Housing, groceries, and transportation are just a few examples where costs are increasing faster than wages. Many of the goals of my generation (baby boomers), such as owning a single-family home with a white picket fence in a cul-de-sac, or the idea of retiring early, sometimes referred to as "freedom 55", now seem out of reach to my kids' generation. It's no wonder young parents have concerns for their children's financial futures. Questions that new parents might be asking themselves are: will my children be able to afford their own homes, how much should I expect to help them financially, or, will they ever have enough money for retirement?

This book presents a quick, simple, powerful, low-cost solution to those concerns by providing all the information busy parents need to create a firm financial foundation for their families throughout their lives. I call it the *Newborn Nest Egg* Formula, and it can safeguard your children's financial future while simultaneously securing your own. The tremendous wealth this formula generates can also provide your children with freedom from limitations as they become adults and pursue their life's ambitions.

Let me be clear, I am not suggesting that wealth is the end goal of our lives; it just provides the energy required to accomplish our most important purposes. Think of your life, and the lives of your kids, as a car taking each of you on a journey to your desired destinations, and money is the fuel your cars need to run on. The important accomplishments you wish to achieve can only be reached by picking the right roads to get you there, but in every case you must have fuel to move forward. You can reach a lot more destinations when you don't have to worry about stopping for gas, or whether you have enough in the tank to get you there.

> **The first societal presumption that must be turned upside down is this: we must stop thinking of using our efforts to create the fuel to power us to our life's goals, and start thinking of wealth as the fuel that self-generates, freeing us to use our energy to accomplish more noble pursuits.**

This may sound like a major undertaking, but it starts with a simple change of mindset and becomes more entrenched and natural as we put the *Newborn Nest Egg* formula into practice. Wise parents initiate a financial foundation for their kids as soon as possible to allow the greatest timespan in which it can grow. This reduces the energy required to generate future wealth to the minimum possible amount. It thereby allows the foundation of wealth to build automatically without impeding the other lifestyle experiences and opportunities that great parents want to provide for their kids as they are growing up. Ultimately, as your children launch into adulthood, having an established financial foundation gives them the freedom to pursue their hopes, dreams, and ambitions without the limitations of financial concerns. They will already have a substantial wealth-building process in place, the wisdom to manage it and add to it, and the confidence to make career and/or business choices without fear of failure.

Both Bill Gates and Warren Buffett, two of the world's wealthiest individuals, and great friends with each other, have talked about giving only small(ish) sums of money to their children. Bill Gates has publicly stated that he plans to give $10 million per child. This decision is part of his belief that leaving too much money to his children would not be good for them and that it is better for them to earn their own success. Warren Buffett has expressed similar sentiments regarding the transfer of wealth to his children. He has stated that his strategy is to give his children "enough money so that they would feel they could do anything, but not so much that they could do nothing."

> **Parents who implement the *Newborn Nest Egg* formula will provide this same benefit for themselves, their children, and future generations: enough wealth to instill the confidence to do anything, but not so much that they could do nothing.**

Amounts that would seem trivial to these billionaires are colossal for many of us, yet still within reach. The wonder of what you're about to learn is how to become such astute parents, able to give your kids million-dollar+ nest eggs while enhancing their drive and ambition. You'll be empowered to provide them with much more than just the money; you'll also gift them the process you have put in place to generate wealth automatically. With this knowledge and financial foundation, your kids will become self-made *multimillionaires* in their lifetimes with virtual certainty, accompanied by the wisdom not to gloat about it, overindulge, or become complacent, but to accomplish great things with it.

We all understand a nest egg to be the funds we need for retirement, and for most people the word retirement means a specific age. I want to challenge that definition and say that retirement is simply when we have enough money to stop working at things we need to do, and start doing only what we love to do. Retirement age is actually a relatively recent concept that was set at age 65 when Social Security was established in 1935 as part of President Roosevelt's New Deal. Retirement doesn't mean we necessarily quit working (that can feel unproductive and unfulfilling), it just means we no longer have to work for financial reasons, so anything we choose to do can be for more noble reasons.

A nest egg will be a different amount for each family. Where you choose to live, your goals and ambitions, and whom you are supporting, all have an impact on this amount. Most adults have an idea of what they consider financial independence or set-for-life. Kids, on the other hand, have no such understanding of money or retirement, nor any concept of how to get there. By the time they reach adulthood, start earning an income, acquire some financial acumen, and put it into practice to start generating their own nest egg, they are most likely in their 30s or beyond, with much less time remaining for any long-term strategy. If their career hasn't taken off or they've faced a setback or two it could lead to a prolonged working life, a financially insecure lifestyle, or even being resigned to poverty during their "golden years". If they don't develop wealth-building goals until their middle years it can lead to desperation-based career planning and investing: chasing the latest trends, fads, and fantastical schemes to make up for the lack of savings. Once reaching this point it's easy to get drawn into the get-rich-quick schemes that are rampant online today, which generally only make money for the purveyors of the schemes, not for the users.

As a new parent, you can free your children from all this potential financial and emotional turmoil by following the *Newborn Nest Egg* formula. It takes three steps:

1. Ensure that your own retirement nest egg process is on track

2. Establish a lucrative wealth-building strategy for your kids immediately

3. Impart wealth-building wisdom to your kids as they grow up

The moment these three steps are committed to (meaning you have taken the necessary actions you'll learn throughout this book to implement them), you have established what I call a 'safety nest' for your family. The term *safety nest* is the fusion of two concepts, a safety net and a nest egg. This synergy provides tremendous lifelong benefits; the total is greater than the sum of its parts.

It can give your kids incredible confidence as they mature into adults, knowing that they are already on track to be financially set-for-life, and for an early retirement from mandatory work. It also provides the freedom to pursue their passions and take a few calculated risks rather than being stuck in a dead-end job they must endure just to make ends meet. It even allows them to make important life decisions that are not limited by financial considerations but reflect their true character and integrity.

Ultimately the *Newborn Nest Egg* formula provides generational wealth, enabling your kids to pass on the same wealth wisdom, security, and financial freedom for generations to come. The objective is to create a sizable nest egg in the future without unduly impeding your family's lifestyle, activities, opportunities, and adventures along the way. This provides the valuable lifelong safety nest with the big golden nest egg at the end. As soon as the *Newborn Nest Egg* formula has been implemented, the recipient can be considered wealthy.

Each of us was raised in a different home and family environment. Some grew up with parents who provided their every need, with lots of lifestyle perks and advantages, while others had a much more financially challenging upbringing where money was always tight. Some even grew up in extremely difficult situations like an uncaring parent or parents, abusive parents, or no parents in the picture at all. Regardless of the economic situation you came from, now that you are a parent, or about to become one, you undoubtedly want to provide your children with at least as much, and probably more, than you experienced. Some new parents are determined to reverse the cycle of poverty and difficulty they grew up in and set a course for generational wealth from this point on. But the cost of living is soaring. The cost of housing particularly is now a greater multiple of annual incomes than it was for past generations. As these trends continue, it will become increasingly difficult for your kids to make it on their own. Your role as provider(s) may not be complete as soon as you have helped them through college, as was often the case in the past. This is where the role of a safety nest comes in. It is the gift of financial freedom and wealth-building wisdom that will allow them to thrive in their adult years and beyond.

Until kids reach their early twenties, their parents are considered financially responsible for them. After that point, people are considered adults and cease to be dependents as far as the IRS is concerned. From then on, financial responsibility shifts from parents to children as they graduate, get jobs, and begin paying their own expenses. Within these 20 years or so, the most important thing parents can do to ensure their kids' lifelong financial success is to impart financial wisdom. The goal of this book is to empower parents with the tools to provide a double-barreled financial foundation for their children: a system that will generate enough money for them to retire comfortably, and the financial acumen to generate much more wealth throughout their lives. This becomes even more critical once you understand the simple and powerful financial juggernaut you will create for your kids. Once you hand over control of the nest egg you have established, your kids must have the financial savvy to manage it so that it operates as the lifelong safety nest it was designed to be.

The power of the *Newborn Nest Egg* formula is that it can create millions of dollars for your family's future with very little of your money, time, or effort; and it will do so with virtual certainty. Once you understand the principles, which are completely covered in this book, it will take less than one hour of your time, just once in your life, not every month or year. And it will only cost about as much as a fast-food meal for your family

once a month. Consider yourself astute if this sounds too good to be true because most claims of this nature are exactly that.

Key to attaining the means to give this extraordinary gift is overcoming two conspicuous roadblocks that society has erected for us and our kids these days. First is the lack of sound wealth-building education provided in most fields of study at our schools, colleges, and universities, and second is the overwhelming onslaught of social media messages proclaiming easy wealth, which are virtually all rubbish. The simple, sound, financial principles taught here will be adequate to overcome the lack of such training included in most school curricula. And the practical applications to follow will empower you to guide your family through the minefield of get-rich-quick schemes that will be incessantly thrust upon them throughout their lives.

It is virtually impossible to escape the onslaught of messages proclaiming quick, easy ways for anyone to get rich overnight. Whether it's social media influencer channels, affiliate marketing, day-trading, cryptocurrencies, NFTs, Reddit crowd power, eCommerce drop-shipping, some AI-based strategy, or any number of "new opportunities". These schemes prey on people who are in financially difficult situations; desperate and willing to try anything. The truth is that if all these approaches were so great, nobody would be so anxious to share them with us; they would just keep the secrets to themselves and operate with fewer competitors. Of course, the reason they advertise their programs so aggressively is to sell us the hype rather than keep performing the strategies themselves. If that doesn't give you much faith in the systems they are peddling, it's because you can see through their motives better than most. You are probably aware that the few examples of remarkable success they present are only a small part of the story. The vast majority of people who try their schemes lose money during the set-up and learning phase, then give up and never make any return on their so-called investment. The most popular online products are just "secrets" or "training" on how to make money with online products. That's the definition of a pyramid scheme, and we all know how those work out.

There are some money-making programs out there that are legitimate and worthwhile, of course; it's just difficult to pick the good ones out of all the noise. This book offers a fundamentally different approach. It teaches a very straightforward, easy way to put a process in place immediately that will create generational wealth with virtual certainty; and not just a little! Everything you need to know is included here; there is no further investment required to learn it or manage it, and it will work for everyone who follows the straightforward steps, not just a few fortunate individuals.

At the opposite end of the wealth-help spectrum are the get-rich-slow schemes. These are the ones marketed by your bank and virtually all other financial institutions. A massive industry has been created to profit from the lack of financial training included in most educational programs. The entire industry is built on peoples' desires to grow a nest egg for themselves and their families without having received sufficient education in financial matters to implement it themselves. Representatives from this industry won't teach you to generate wealth yourself, nor will they generate much wealth for you, because their systems are set up primarily to make themselves rich, not you. These are large corporations whose main objective is to maximize their own revenue and profits; we are simply the potential customers for their products. Have you ever wondered why you can have meetings with financial planners at the bank for free? It wouldn't be a viable business model if they weren't finding ways to make money. You will soon realize what's going on behind the curtain and learn simple ways to avoid that whole industry and its associated fees.

This book is written for new parents who want to provide a safety nest for their children, which we have defined as the combination of foundational wealth with ongoing wealth-building wisdom. Prudent parents want an honest but powerful way to give their kids financial independence, but also provide something worth much more than just the money. That's because the gift of a sizable lump-sum of money can often be destructive. It's like giving someone a very powerful machine without the instructions and training to operate it safely. A real nest egg must include the knowledge, coaching, and motivation for your kids to carry on increasing their own wealth, and ultimately creating generational wealth.

Well, you might say, doesn't every parent want the ability to give their kids this kind of nest egg? In one way, yes, but in a more important way, maybe not. It depends on their definition of the most inconspicuous word in that sentence, the word *"want"*. Sure, every new parent might *want* to get a jump on providing wealth for their kids in the sense of, "yup, that would be nice", but the definition of *want* that almost nobody will act on is the kind that would be understood in this sentence: you can be a professional athlete if you really *want* to! That's because being a professional athlete isn't something that just happens to you. It doesn't just work out that way if you have a casual or passive interest in it. You gotta ***want*** it! It must be a very high priority for you. You need to be proactive in pursuing your dream with a passion. You have to put in the work, the hours, the practice, get the best coaching and advice from experienced athletes, give up a lot of the free-time activities that other people your age are enjoying, and instead get your satisfaction from pursuing your dream.

For example, Serena Williams holds the most major singles, doubles, and mixed doubles titles combined among all active tennis players in the world. As a child, she used books and videos for instruction and began practicing at three years old on a court near her home in Compton, California. She became a professional tennis player in 1995 and won the French Open, the U.S. Open, and Wimbledon in 2002, defeating her sister Venus in the finals of each tournament. She won her first Australian Open in 2003, making her one of only six women in the Open era to complete a Career Grand Slam. In 2008, she won the U.S. Open and teamed with Venus to capture a second women's doubles Olympic gold medal at the Beijing Games. Serena is also the only professional tennis player to accomplish a Career Golden Slam in singles & doubles. In December 2015 she was named Sportsperson of the Year by Sports Illustrated magazine.

Stephen (Steph) Curry started playing basketball at the age of seven. He was named all-state, all-conference, and team MVP while he was 16, and led his high school team to three conference titles and three state playoff appearances. Through three seasons at college, Steph continued to excel and broke all kinds of records. He is now entering his 16th season in the NBA and has achieved 4 NBA championships and too many other awards and scoring records to count. He is the NBA career 3-pointer leader with 3,747, and counting, and the only player to score over 400, 3-pointers in a season. In 2022 he was named Sports Illustrated Sportsperson of the Year, and is widely considered the best shooter in NBA history. How does Steph maintain the superhuman brilliance we get to witness whenever he's on the court? He shoots a minimum of 2,000 shots a week, typically more like 500 per day, including 100 in warmup just before the game. We might see him drain 10, 3-pointers in a game, but behind that is a lifetime of practice. If we consider his minimum of 2,000 shots per week since high school, that's well over two million practice shots!

> **The two common factors that made each of these athletes into Sportsperson of the Year, literally the best in the world at the time, are these: start early, and remain resolute.**

Creating a nest egg for your kids requires the same early timing, and the same commitment to never stop following the simple process you are about to learn. If you *want* to generate substantial wealth for your kids, with enough determination that you will take action now, and remain committed for the long haul, this book will show you how. You will see that it is *much* easier to become wealthy than to become a professional athlete, plus it is not limited to just a few exceptional performers. The difference is that getting rich is about working smart, not working hard, whereas for athletes there is no substitute for hard work. There are similarities in the required attitude though, and most people won't do the smart, simple things necessary to become wealthy. They will instead find excuses, claim that their circumstances don't allow it, put off getting started until it is too late, assume they already know a better way, or live beyond their means to give the impression of being wealthy while their lifestyle is really a sham. Don't let that be you or your family!

Helping your kids become wealthy won't be expensive, complicated, or time-consuming, but it may be hard because it requires you to change your lifestyle in a small way, remain disciplined, and never drift back into your old ways.

Regardless of your age as parents you must rise above the adolescent aversion to doing hard things, and you must teach this principle to your kids as they mature into adults. There is no need to do hard things just to prove a point, as some personality types tend to do; it's much better to do valuable things in as smart and efficient a way as possible. It's the results that count, not the effort. All you will need to succeed is the fortitude to take 100% responsibility for your results - no *blaming* and no *complaining!*

You can use the *Newborn Nest Egg* formula for each of your kids at any age, but the earlier you get started the less it will cost and the more wealth you will generate. You can also use this book as an easy way to pass along the necessary wealth wisdom to your kids as you transition the monetary portion of their nest egg. In addition, at about the age of 16, give them the next book in the series which can be found at www.FastWealth.com. This *Newborn Nest Egg* book includes a bit more background, teaching the financial fundamentals that are not part of school curricula, whereas the companion book is a very practical guide full of money-making ideas for young adults. It describes the *FAST Wealth* formula; the fastest and most assured formula for creating their own wealth-building powerhouse early in their career.

Almost every promoter of a money-making scheme will tell you that anyone can do it. The *Newborn Nest Egg* **formula is fundamentally different because** *everyone* **can do it.**

Motivation

So, what motivated me to write this book? The simple answer is that I did all the wrong things early in my career, and early in the life of my family. I thought I could work hard enough and smart enough to make all the money my family would need. I tried way too many ventures, both in business and investing, hoping for the big win; and when I did succeed a few times, I took excessive risks with my financial gains and almost lost it all. When I finally got to the point of analyzing what I should have done instead, I developed and began successfully using the investment strategies I am presenting here. I didn't study finance, economics, business administration, or accounting in school, but I finally mastered the ability to generate and accumulate wealth from the income of a fairly ordinary career. My training and profession were in engineering. I started out earning about sixteen thousand dollars per year. Today that would be well below minimum wage. Now I am free from day-to-day work but earn more from my investments than I ever did in salary. And this is now passive income; all I have to do to earn it is live my life.

I learned the practical lessons of successful financial management from the world of real dollars and cents, not classes and professors. I call it my Street MBA. I progressed in the business world from a hands-on designer of electronic systems to manager of an engineering department, and then to senior corporate management positions, a member of the C-suite with Profit & Loss (P&L) responsibilities; always having to "live and die by the numbers". I even started a couple of companies from the ground up in which I was CEO. One of them I took public through an IPO (not a big one like those that make the financial news), and the other I sold to a venture capital group. I have bought and sold other companies and have been President of corporate business divisions, both as an employee and as a consultant. But these endeavors were **not** what made me financially independent; it was the principles I am now sharing with you. My career certainly produced some windfall profits a few times, but when I took risks with those funds I ended up with losses as often as gains. I never held fast to my earnings, and got them generating recurring passive income for me, until I developed and committed to the investment formula presented in this book.

I am currently Chairman of the finance committee of a charitable organization with several thousand members and multimillion-dollar annual budgets. I am also Chairman of another foundation that holds real estate assets in the range of $100 million in value for use in non-profit endeavors to serve those in need. These are unpaid positions, but they are my way of giving back out of gratitude, and helping those who simply didn't have the opportunities or experiences I had. Taking the roles of highest financial responsibility in these organizations obviously would not be prudent, nor would I have been elected to do so, if I didn't have a demonstrated ability to wisely and shrewdly manage finances and high-value assets.

At various stages of managing my personal finances, I used the services of stockbrokers, bank financial planners, private wealth advisors, subscription investment-advisory services, and numerous online systems that promised extraordinary returns. All of these taught me very valuable lessons, but they were expensive lessons. When I analyzed all my costs versus the returns that were being generated for me, I determined that my advisors were making as much from my money as I was. That didn't seem very efficient, but I realized that I lacked the knowledge and experience to do it myself. When I took control of every aspect of my finances and developed the formula for simple, straightforward, almost guaranteed high-end gains, and stuck to my own program, I finally became a multimillionaire with foundational wealth that keeps on growing. Now I have the freedom to set my own schedule, travel, consult, teach classes and seminars, volunteer, spend lots of time with my family and friends, and write books.

The reason I'm writing this book is certainly not for the money; most books of this nature barely pay back the publishing costs. My greatest motivation is the realization that it wasn't primarily the income from my career that made me financially independent (and I never worked anywhere that provided me a pension), it was the insights and strategies you are about to learn, and this book gives me the privilege of sharing them with you. It was indeed my career that enabled me (almost forced me) to develop the *Newborn Nest Egg* formula, but I realize now that I could have achieved even more wealth with an ordinary job if I had known these principles and techniques and started using them from a younger age.

Another motivation for me is the fact that I have already been teaching this formula for over sixteen years to numerous younger individuals, and I get great satisfaction from observing how well it works for them. One aspect of the charitable work I now do, along with my wife, is mentoring young couples who are preparing for marriage. Financial security is a very important aspect of a successful marriage, especially for starting a family. The principles of the *Newborn Nest Egg* formula are exactly what we teach these young couples. One such example is our son and his wife. They got married right after college and went from starting their careers with a negative net worth, due to student loans, to having a net worth of over a million dollars in just over seven years. They also have the *Newborn Nest Egg* formula already set up to generate multimillion-dollar nest eggs for each of their newborn kids.

The structure of this book is straightforward. It is divided into four upcoming chapters that provide some background and financial principles that must be understood before initiating the *Newborn Nest Egg* formula. These are the strategies that first need to be understood by you, the parents, and then imparted to your kids as they develop and mature into adults. The foundational principles are followed by a chapter that presents the step-by-step process for implementing the formula. The last chapter provides an overview of the results that can be anticipated by following the formula. Appendix A presents a comparison of results that could be expected from alternative strategies.

The background concepts may seem less important, and some readers will already know some of them, but they are very valuable in terms of confidently implementing the steps of the formula. If you were to follow the steps blindly you would likely lack the confidence to hold the course long-term, and could easily be swayed by doubts or the directions that others take. Also, when you know what's ahead it's worth the effort to work through the background. These principles will give you confidence that you are following the right formula, not something you will try for a while and then look for alternatives. Eventually, the entire contents of this book will need to be understood by your kids, readying them to receive and carry on managing the sizable foundation of wealth you will be initiating for them.

Although this book will show you step-by-step how to generate a lot of wealth for your family for generations, it is not simply a book about money. It is primarily a book about great parenting. It will stretch your goals as new parents by advocating the provision of financial security and acumen for your children throughout their lives and even to future generations. Money is the key topic simply because it is the most powerful tool you have to provide safety and security for your children as you start your parenting journey. And money is also the most powerful means of providing freedom from limitations as your children develop, mature, and pursue their life's ambitions. A lifelong journey of increasing wealth and financial stability provides an ever-present light at the end of the tunnel. When a person's financial future always looks brighter than today, it can make many of life's challenges a lot less daunting.

CHAPTER 2

WEALTH WISDOM

The Most Valuable Resource

T hink about the following question for a few minutes before you read ahead to find the answer – what is one thing your kids have more of right now than almost anyone else in the world? To give you some time to think about this, I won't answer it right away. Instead, I'll provide some hints to help you try to solve it yourself. They currently possess something of great financial value, and most others, including yourself, have less of it. You probably don't realize how much monetary value this commodity has. It's somewhat equivalent to owning a big bar of pure gold, and your kids' bars are a lot bigger than most other peoples' gold bars. The thing is that neither you, nor most other people, realize that they already own this gold, and don't know how to turn it into money that can actually be spent on the things they will consider to be important in life. You might think I'm talking about an intangible form of wealth like family, love, or a rich cultural heritage. Those are all great things, and in many ways they have more value than money, but I'm talking about something that your kids possess a lot of right now that literally has a high financial, monetary value.

Have you figured it out yet? What your kids possess more of than most people in the world is youth! They have more time ahead of them. In business, this amount of time in front of us is often called runway. Your kids possess this runway of time simply because they are younger than most other people. And this time factor has a great deal of real financial value, as you'll learn shortly. In fact, the *Newborn Nest Egg* formula simply wouldn't work reliably without it. As new parents, you also have a significant time runway in front of you, and it can still be used to grow your own nest egg using the same principles.

The best wealth-growing strategy for people with a lot of youth is a long-term system, which means strategies that may be more suitable for those with a short time horizon will not be appropriate. It also means that for the *Newborn Nest Egg* formula, it is critical to find long-lasting opportunities, only those that will work for multiple decades. The good news is that these can be found with confidence, and because they are known to be durable and reliable they are also safe and provide powerful wealth-building properties.

The following sections present the key aspects of personal wealth management that are very important for parents to learn, put into practice, and then pass on to their kids during the first twenty-some years of their lives. With this knowledge, your children will be able to take over and grow the nest egg you will be gifting to them, and turn it into generational wealth for your grandchildren and beyond.

Hire Money to Work for You

A key weakness of our education system, as mentioned earlier, is it doesn't teach the fundamentals of money management unless we get a degree in finance or business administration. Even a professional degree seldom equips the graduate for personal wealth creation, or even owning and operating their own business. Simply relying on the school system to teach your children about wealth creation and money management is therefore not a good approach. The assumption it leaves us with is that the path to success is: work hard, study hard, get into the best college or university, work and study hard some more, and then eventually get a good job and start climbing the corporate ladder. There is nothing wrong with this path if it interests you, you are good at it, can afford it, and don't mind starting to earn money later in life, often with a negative net worth due to student loan debt.

The inevitable result of this assumption, however, is that you work through all this career preparation in order to work for your money. Presumably the harder you work in school, the better your education will be, and the more money you can earn by working for somebody else, or for some corporation, throughout your career. It's OK if that's what you want to experience in life, but it is not likely to be the best way to get rich if it's all you do.

It is far better to get your money working for you than for you to just work for your money all your life. Let's take a look at what this entails.

First of all, the two are not mutually exclusive. In fact, a primary source of income is absolutely necessary in order to have some money to put to work. In reality, to become wealthy with an ordinary job or career you have to do both. Initially, you have to work for your money, but as soon as possible, and as much as possible, get that money you are working for to start working for you.

> **You will soon learn how each $2,000 you get working for you can reliably earn over $1 million – and do so completely passively. But you can even start with $0.00 and just invest a small monthly amount to achieve the same results.**

Secondly, working for your money almost always has certain limitations. If you work for wages, you will likely start out at minimum wage. That will make it difficult (but not impossible) to create much of a nest egg for yourself or your kids. If you or your spouse are currently working for minimum wage, don't despair; the second book in this series can teach you the *FAST Wealth* formula which includes numerous approaches to increasing your income as well as your wealth (note that those are two separate things). If you work for wages but get into something that requires a skill, or provides on-the-job training, it will usually result in earning more income, hopefully at least what the average full-time worker earns. You will soon see how this can be enough to create generous nest eggs if you know how to make money grow. If you and/or your spouse earn a professional's income you should have no problem finding enough money to put to work, as long as you have the right attitude, the knowledge to do it wisely, and the motivation to start now and never quit until you're rich.

Even a good education and the resulting career won't make you very rich if all you do is work for your money. Let's say that you chose the path of becoming a professional of some kind. This could mean you become an accountant, lawyer, marketer, advertising specialist, salesperson, business manager, computer programmer, architect, engineer, etc. In this case you can generally earn a very respectable salary, but that salary alone won't make you rich. Earning a salary sounds more sophisticated than hourly wages, but it often means you have to work very long hours for no extra pay. To be good at your job and climb the corporate ladder you'll often be required to work way more than 40 hours per week. That's because you will be competing with all the other aggressive young professionals who all want the same promotion. It puts a lot of pressure on most people, and they often end up burned out instead of successfully reaching the upper ranks of management where they can delegate most of their menial work and focus on the big picture. And even that won't make them very rich if they don't get their money working for them as well. As Robert Frost, American poet and winner of four Pulitzer Prizes said, "By working faithfully eight hours a day, you may eventually get to be a boss and work twelve hours a day".

A friend of mine went into accounting; he even got an MBA. When accountants first start working there is a period much like an internship before they write their CPA exam and receive their designation to practice professionally. It's a lot like a doctor doing a residency or a lawyer before they pass the Bar. During this time of gaining experience and studying to write the licensing exam, these educated professionals are treated a bit like fraternity pledges; they are given all the grunt work to do and expected to put in ridiculous hours. My friend did a calculation of how much he was earning after receiving his advanced degree but before passing his CPA exam. It came out to around $6 per hour because he was working up to 16 hours per day for a meager salary at that time. When the boss said, "Have that report on my desk by tomorrow morning", when do you think that work had to be done? Overnight! During tax season, even senior accountants work seven days a week, 16 hours per day, without any additional pay.

Whether you earn wages or salary, there is a cap – a maximum amount you are likely to earn. That's because in any job you will always be doing something that others are willing and able to do for a similar amount of money. There are a few exceptions to the wage and salary caps, but they are very rare. Corporate CEOs of the biggest and best companies in the world do earn exceptional amounts of money; millions of dollars per year. The best sports superstars or celebrities also earn what seems like obscene amounts of money, but they are worth every penny. That's because they also earn exceptional amounts of money for those who employ them, sponsor them, or ride in their wakes. These individuals are unique. There is no one else like them; nobody who can do exactly what they do or be who they are – so they have no direct competitors. If their services are in high demand, they have tremendous earning power for themselves and for everyone associated with them. This book will not teach anyone how to become one of them, but if your kid happens to become such a mega-earner, at least they will know how to handle their money wisely. How many tragic stories have you heard of those who got rich too quickly and easily and then blew it all, often on excessive partying? Then they ended up broke and in rehab.

I bought a small business once that used a contract bookkeeping service. I kept using the same service provider for a couple of years because the firm knew all the financial details of the company, which was important during the transition of ownership. Near the end of the second year, however, I let them know that I would be getting quotes from other bookkeepers, but I gave them a chance to provide me with a competitive bid as well. By this time, I was much more organized with my financial documentation and accounts than the previous owner had ever been, so bookkeeping was far easier and quicker than it had been in the past. I received several quotes, all of which were lower than what I was paying the original bookkeeping service. The best-and-final bid I received from the original bookkeepers was to keep their prices the same. I pointed out the reduced workload, which they acknowledged, and asked why they couldn't reduce their price. The response was that they didn't price according to effort but according to value, and they perceived the value to be the same as ever. What they didn't seem to consider was that other equally qualified professionals were willing to do the work for less. I switched to a new bookkeeping service and saved 75%. This is the kind of limit that everyone who works for their money has to contend with.

The truth is that it is not necessary to be a celebrity, reach upper management positions, or own a successful business in order to create generational wealth. Anyone who earns a decent wage as a skilled or semi-skilled employee, or pretty much any level of professional salary, can do it. Most people won't though, and the reason is that they're conditioned to work for their money instead of putting their money to work for them. They focus on getting the next salary increase or promotion, or starting a business of their own, instead of learning to wisely manage the income they already earn. That strategy is severely limiting, whereas putting your money to work has no such limit.

Do not take any of this as advice for you or your kids not to go to college or university. There are many benefits to having a good education, and the college experience can add to a person's fulfillment and social opportunities in life. The point is that if you chose not to, or didn't get the privilege of going to college for whatever reason, you can still provide generational wealth for your family as long as you understand the simple financial principles you are learning right now. Let's look at how much more powerful it is to get your money working for you instead of just working for your money.

Getting your money working for you is, by definition, investing. This is a key area where our education system typically provides little to no background; it leaves people in the dark about where and how to make wise investments. Most people therefore feel inadequate, uninformed, ill-equipped, gullible, uneasy, foolish, and generally lost when it comes to making investment decisions. Without a solid understanding of investment strategies, these are completely rational and coherent beliefs. The truth is that most people *will* lose money on investments without the guidance of trained advisors, but those advisors are expensive. One of the largest industries in the world exists solely to profit from this gap in people's knowledge. It is called the financial planning or wealth management industry, and in the US alone it employs over a million people, all earning sizable salaries, commissions, bonuses, and perks. With the right formula, you can bypass that entire industry and all its expenses, and confidently get your own money working for you and your family.

When money is working for you, there is no salary cap – no limit to how much it can earn. Think of each invested dollar as another employee who works for you 24 x 7, never needs to sleep, never takes a sick day, mental health day, or caregiver-leave, doesn't arrive at work late and leave early, doesn't get injured, doesn't require vacation pay or health insurance, doesn't go on strike or demand a pay raise, doesn't get into a funk and start drinking too much, doesn't argue with other employees, and doesn't get old, tired, and unproductive (ask me how I know). If you have ever had employees, or even watched your co-workers and managers interact, you will appreciate immediately how great an employee your *money* can be compared to some *people*. Money can earn passive income, that is, income that just accumulates in your account without you having to do anything except wait. Any kind of successful investing creates this exact situation, and that's what it means to get your money working for you. We'll talk more about it in subsequent chapters but first, let's figure out how to assign enough money to work for you to generate that nest egg you want for your family. Here is a hint: it's not necessarily a lump sum amount you need to accumulate, just a small monthly commitment will do.

Net Worth

I'm not a great fan of the term *net worth* because it conveys the impression that the ultimate worth of an individual is a financial value. Obviously the true worth of a person is not in how much money they have. We all have an equal intrinsic value as human beings. But the term has a specific definition in finance-speak, so let's be sure to understand what it means.

In financial terms, a person's net worth is the sum total of all their assets, minus all their liabilities. Assets are what you own, and liabilities are what you owe. Since assets and liabilities can be in many different forms, all of them must be represented in dollars (or whatever currency you are working in) so that addition and subtraction can be done for all components in the same units of measure. Assets can be anything of monetary value such as cash, stocks, bonds, real estate, vehicles, furniture, collectibles, jewelry, precious metals, etc. These are all measured, if possible, or estimated if a definitive measurement is not possible, and then added together and represented as a dollar amount. Liabilities must similarly be quantified in dollar amounts, and most of them are precisely measurable because they are defined in dollar terms. They can be things like mortgages, personal loans, student loans, car loans, credit card debt, unpaid taxes, and the like. It is very unusual for an individual to have any liabilities that are not debts or payables denominated in terms of currency, i.e., dollars.

For example, if you had a house worth $500,000, a car worth $50,000, cash savings of $50,000, investments worth $50,000, and another $50,000 worth of furniture, appliances, electronic devices, and jewelry, your total assets would be $700,000. If your mortgage owing was $350,000, your car loan was $30,000, you had a personal loan of $20,000, and credit card debt of $5,000, your total liabilities would be $405,000. Your net worth would therefore be $700,000 - $405,000 = $295,000. When this net worth number becomes $1,000,000, you are officially a millionaire. That's the size of nest egg you can readily provide for each of your children, and likely several times that amount.

The point of knowing and calculating these numbers is to help you determine how to structure your lifestyle to increase the net worth you can provide for your family in a fast and predictable manner. In the example above, the personal loan and credit card debt would very likely cost a lot more in monthly interest payments than the cash savings would earn in a bank account. That's because credit card interest rates are typically 16% to 22% annualized, and personal loans can easily be 10% to 12%, whereas the interest being earned on cash in a savings account is usually a paltry 2% to 3%. Simply paying these loans off with the cash savings could increase your net worth quite quickly. The car loan may be another opportunity to reduce monthly expenses, thus further increasing your net worth if you invest the equivalent of those monthly payments.

There is one more way to look at an asset, and thus at the net worth you are creating for your children, and that is in terms of its future value. For example, if you make a loan to someone that won't be paid back until 30 years from now, according to accounting principles you can still count the full amount of the loan as an asset today, even though you will not have the cash available to spend until the 30 years is up. If you set a process in place now that will reliably generate a million dollars for your child's retirement, it can similarly be considered an asset today. Keep this in mind for later chapters.

A Dollar Saved is Two Dollars Earned

There is an old saying that goes something like, "a penny saved is a penny earned". I believe this proverb came from way back in jolly old England when a penny was a sizable chunk of change, both figuratively and literally. At that time an English penny could buy something of value like perhaps a loaf of bread, so it had some buying power. It was also quite a large metal coin about the size of an American silver dollar, so it was hefty. Regardless of the details, the principle still holds today, only it's a lot more impactful than it sounds.

In the modern world we could modify the old saying to "a dollar saved is a dollar earned" but it's not true anymore. In reality, it's more like a dollar saved is two dollars earned. The reason is that for every dollar on the price tag of an item, we actually need to earn about two dollars to buy it. We'll do some simple math to show that this is essentially the case.

Let's say that you want to buy a new TV that's priced at $2,000. How much would you need to earn to pay for it? For this example, we'll use a hypothetical $100,000 as your annual salary, in which case you will have up to 35% deducted for federal income tax, state income tax, social security, and Medicare. Your take-home pay would therefore only be about 65% of what you earn. Now when you go to pay for the TV, State and local sales taxes can add up to another 10% or more. If you buy any kind of extended warranty for the TV you will spend another 10% to 20% of the cost for that. Over $4,000 of your $100,000 salary will therefore have been used up in the process of buying this $2,000 TV! As another example, let's say you go out to a restaurant and order menu items that total $100. When you pay for services like this it can be a similar burden on your earnings because you start with after-tax income, pay sales taxes of up to 10%, plus leave a gratuity of 16% to 20% on top of the $100 plus tax. So, you will literally have to earn about two dollars in wages or salary for every dollar listed on a price tag or menu. This situation becomes even more acute when your income puts you into a higher tax bracket where you pay a greater percentage of your earnings as income taxes.

Let's think about this from another angle. If you work very hard to get a pay raise or promotion, how much is the extra income really worth? If your salary is hypothetically $100,000 per year, and you got a 10% pay raise, that's $10,000 more per year. That feels great, right? Unfortunately, it is likely to bump you up into a higher income tax bracket, so your employer now has to withhold a greater percentage of your pay and remit it to the government. Your take-home pay therefore doesn't go up by $10,000 but by approximately $6,300 per year, or $525 per month. That's something, but it's not worth much more than just foregoing a couple of $2,000 discretionary purchases per year. In other words, if you focus only on getting a raise or promotion it will never make you very rich. You will still be working for your money instead of getting your money working for you.

> **The point of the above examples is to make it clear that cost-saving is about twice as powerful as getting a pay raise in terms of assigning more money to work for you and your family. Plus, cost-saving is a process you have great control over, whereas getting a raise is primarily in someone else's hands.**

In fact, without learning how to save, it will be impossible to make the commitments necessary for successful investing. The income you make right now will be enough to generate a million-dollar nest egg for your kids if you commit to always spending less than you earn. The concept of saving entails two aspects, each as valuable as the other. First is the idea of cost-saving. This means cutting costs wherever you can. Second is the concept of setting funds aside and investing them instead of spending them. In the next chapter, you will start to see in more detail how to get this source of funds to start working for you.

CHAPTER 3

BOUNTY BY BUDGET

T he strategy being presented in this book requires assigning a small to medium amount of your money every month to work for you. Think of it as continuously hiring more of the greatest kind of employees. You will see shortly the amounts required to reach the goals you set for yourself. For some readers, the ability to contribute a few percent of their income every month to provide a safety nest for their kids might seem next to impossible, while for others it would not be much of a stretch at all. If you are in the position of having difficulty finding any leftover cheddar at the end of the month, this section of the book will be very useful to help find the money. On the other hand, if shuffling a few bucks per month into investments is not a significant challenge for you, read this section more as lessons that can be taught to your kids. Either way, there are important principles in terms of both financial management and discipline to be learned, put into practice, and ultimately passed on to your children.

It is not practical to provide specific instances that cover all financial situations, so extrapolation will be necessary by each reader to convert the numbers used here into your individual circumstance. I will present an example based on approximately the average household income in America and demonstrate that this is adequate to implement the *Newborn Nest Egg* formula to create a substantial safety nest for your family.

Before you can put money to work, you must structure your lifestyle to support the commitments you are making. This means providing not only for the milestones your kids will attain on the road to becoming adults (education, extracurricular activities, travel, graduations, wedding, etc.) but establishing a nest egg program for them as well. It is no secret that life is very expensive already, and no mystery that it will become ever more so for the next generation. When I was a kid, a large waterfront home was called a $40,000 mansion. Today the average house price in America is over ten times that amount. It's hard to imagine, but not hard to calculate, that kids being born today will be living in million-dollar homes when they have families of their own, and those will not even be the extravagant houses. The good news is that the same forces that propel higher pricing are even more powerful at driving wealth generation if harnessed correctly.

> **The secret to keeping ahead of all these expenses is to put your money to work, which means always spending less than you make and wisely investing the difference. So, the two steps you must unconditionally commit to are: 1) generating a surplus of funds every month, and 2) investing your surplus wisely.**

You may not have ultimate control over your income, but you do have control and responsibility for all your spending. The first step to controlling spending is to make a budget. Naturally that sounds awful to many people, but this is where the principle of doing hard things, as long as they are valuable, is absolutely necessary. A budget is critical because it reinforces the fact that everything has a trade-off. If you spend more on one item or category, you simply must spend less on another, or you will go into debt, and eventually go broke. The good news is that proper budgeting isn't all that hard, and it doesn't have to take much time or be repeated over and over again.

The following table shows a simple budget format. I may refer to it as your budget but clearly, it is a sample only, and yours may contain different line items and vastly different numbers. The structure of this sample is what's important because it is easy for you to reproduce if you aren't already doing more thorough budgeting in a program or app of some kind. You can download the spreadsheet used for this sample by visiting the website associated with this book, www.Newb ornNestEgg.com. The advantage of the format is that it has a percentage column for each line item. This makes your budget both insightful and self-governing. It is insightful because it shows immediately where your biggest income and expense items are. Those line items are where any changes will have the greatest impact. It is self-governing because it can be easily adjusted to keep the percentages the same whenever your income changes or you decide to change any of your expenses. Once your budget is documented it will be trivial to make changes, which should only be necessary about once per year to continue providing good insights for making your financial decisions.

The sample budget below is based on the income from both parents working, but each earning less than the average full-time worker in

America. This is intended to demonstrate that a Newborn Nest Egg of at least a million dollars can readily be created with approximately the average household income.

The Remainder, or bottom line, of your budget is the amount of money you can employ to work for you. It can be divided up however you see fit between adding to your own retirement nest egg and the safety nest you are building for your children. The objective is to get this bottom line as large as possible without impeding your realistic lifestyle costs. A budget does you no good whatsoever if you don't live by it. If you simply can't live by it, that's equally without value. Make your budget livable but then commit to spending only what you have budgeted, and to investing the bottom line without fail. You will see in subsequent chapters how little it takes to achieve audacious goals when you start early.

Sample Family Budget				
	Annual	Monthly	%	Notes & Suggestions
Income				
Take-Home Income	78000	6500	100.00	Wages or salary of both spouses combined
Estimated Commish		0	-	If part of your income is from commissions
Estimated Gratuities		0	-	If part of your income is from gratuities
Estimated Bonuses		0	-	If part of your income is from bonuses
Side Hustle		0	-	If part of your income is from side hustles
Other		0	-	If you have a second job or side business
Total Income	78000	6500	100.00	
Fixed Costs				
Extra Tax Provision		0	-	Provision for Income taxes on variable income
Mortgage	18000	1500	23.08	Or rent - if you don't own your property
Property Taxes	3000	250	3.85	If you own a home
Car Payment	3600	300	4.62	If you have financed the purchase of a vehicle
Gas	3600	300	4.62	Or charging fees if you drive an EV
Car Maint & Repair	2400	200	3.08	Maintenance is the cheapest way to avoid repairs
Parking	0	0	-	If you pay to park at work, residence, or elsewhere
Phones	900	75	1.15	Including any extra usage fees
Utilities	4800	400	6.15	Electricity, heat, water, trash collection, etc.
Groceries	4800	400	6.15	What you spend to eat at home
Clothing	960	80	1.23	What you need to wear to work & social situations
Personal Hygiene	600	50	0.77	The necessities to keep clean and healthy
Insurance	4200	350	5.38	Vehicle, Life, Health, Home, Contents
Health Care	1200	100	1.54	Medical, Dental, Vision
Child Care	2400	200	3.08	If necessary, so that both parents can work
Medication	600	50	0.77	Prescriptions, Vitamins, Supplements, Etc.
Charitable Donations	4800	400	6.15	Give more because it's tax-deductible
Discretionary Costs				
Education	300	25	0.38	Tuition, Books, Courses, Classes, Online
Furniture	900	75	1.15	Spread out over years to acquire the necessities
Appliances	900	75	1.15	Spread out over years to acquire the necessities
Vehicles	1200	100	1.54	Additional Car, Bike, Motorbike, Scooter, etc.
Electronics	900	75	1.15	Home Entertainment, Computers, Tablets
Subscriptions	600	50	0.77	Streaming services, Amazon/Costco Shopping
Restaurants	1500	125	1.92	Dining out, Coffee shops, Pubs, Fast Food
Entertainment	900	75	1.15	Movies, Concerts, Theater, Golf, Sports Events
Taxi / Uber	600	50	0.77	Any transportation aside from your own vehicle
Travel / Vacation	2100	175	2.69	Trips out of town, except business travel
Gifts	900	75	1.15	Birthdays, Holidays, Weddings
Exercise / Activity	600	50	0.77	Gym Membership, Sports Equipment
Fashions	600	50	0.77	Clothing beyond the basics for everyday wear
Hairstyling	600	50	0.77	Basic haircuts & any additional styling
Cosmetics	600	50	0.77	Products or services beyond basic hygiene
Jewelry	600	50	0.77	Watches, Rings, Necklaces, Piercings, Tattoos
Alcohol	600	50	0.77	Consumed at home or brought to parties
Tobacco / Vaping	0	0	-	Get this down to zero if you possibly can
Contingency	3900	325	5.00	For anything unexpected: ~5% of Income
Total Expenses	74160	6180	95.08	
Remainder	3840	320	4.92	Keep this as high as possible for Investment

Your circumstances may be vastly different from those presented in the sample budget. Of course, you already know that nothing worthwhile is easy, so figure out your own budget as it applies to your situation. If you and your spouse earn less than the average full-time worker, you will need to cut costs more aggressively and/or find ways to increase your income. If you are a single parent, it will be even more challenging, but you can still successfully create a safety nest. Ideas for both cost-saving and additional income generation will be presented shortly. If you earn significantly more than the average, don't be complacent, thinking you don't need to cut costs or find ways to earn more. Shoot for a younger age for your own retirement. Shoot for a greater net worth by retirement age. Generate greater nest eggs for your kids. Provide enough generational wealth that even your grandkids are assured of a safety nest. Generate enough wealth to generously help others who are less fortunate.

Your wealth does not depend on how much you earn but on how much you keep.

I knew the owner of a significant size limousine company in a major American city. He had a fleet of about 70 cars that generated close to $10 million per year in revenue. At first glance he seemed to be doing very well, but in actuality he somehow always spent every dollar he brought in each month and never had any net profit. The reason is that he was always juggling debts and had terrible cash management strategies. He was forever desperate to collect the next few dollars so he could keep his creditors off his back. For example, his cash flow was so dire that when corporate clients would pay their monthly invoices, which could be a couple of thousand dollars each, he would pay to have their checks couriered to him for same-day delivery, costing something like $100 per check. This practice alone cost him probably 2% of his entire revenue. A company like his might normally be able to generate about 10% profit margin, but when you take away 2% of revenue, the profits are already reduced by 20%. That is, they would have been if his company was earning the industry average, but in his case, the costs of debt and cash management seemed to eat up all his profit - a devastating business practice. The key to budgeting in preparation for implementing the *Newborn Nest Egg* formula can be summarized very simply.

Do not spend what you need to live on, and then invest the remainder. Instead, commit to a bottom-line dollar amount for investing and then live on what's left.

Debt: The Good, the Bad, and the Ugly

According to Creighton University's Center for Marriage and Family, debt is the leading cause of strife for the newly married. That's one huge reason to avoid debt, and it's a strong indicator that having a solid wealth-building plan can have the opposite, very positive, effect on your most intimate relationship. In general, debt is the death of wealth! It is easily the most insidious culprit in preventing wealth creation. It is like a drug that addict its user and then destroys their life. The craving for possessions, experiences, image, prestige, or acceptance can be overpowering. Debt can seem like the solution for instant gratification while pushing the consequences out of mind and into some unspecified future. Once a person, or a couple, starts down this road it is very difficult to escape. Paying interest on borrowed money is the antithesis of investing; it's your money working *against* you instead of working *for* you. For these reasons, debt should be avoided in almost every situation. That being said, some debt works against you more powerfully than others. We'll call the least offensive kind "*good debt*" but note that it is not always good.

Astute readers will have noticed that there are two line items in the sample budget for what could be considered debt payments; one is a mortgage, and the other a car loan. These examples represent one type of good debt and one type of bad debt. The key difference is quite simple: Good debt applies to appreciating assets, and bad debt applies to depreciating assets. We will go one step further and talk about ugly debt. This is the worst possible kind, where there is no asset underlying the debt at all, just payments on borrowed money that has already been spent and cannot be recovered by selling an associated asset.

Good debt is misunderstood by a lot of people, and the concept is virtually never taught in school, not until university business classes at least, and even then it applies more to corporate debt than personal debt. It is considered common knowledge in our society that you should always pay off your mortgage as quickly as possible so you can have more discretionary cash for living the good life or saving for retirement. For most people, with typical education and investing experience, this is good advice because at least it's safe. That's because a mortgage is not *always* debt on an *appreciating* asset. In fact, the underlying cause of the worst global financial crisis of our time was the incorrect assumption that real estate *always* increases in value. A mortgage is only good debt if it is structured in a way that ensures you will never owe more than the property is worth. That way you will never lose your house but can own it long-term, regardless of housing value fluctuations. Over long time periods, real estate does generally appreciate in value; in fact, it's difficult to find any real estate anywhere that is currently less expensive than it was twenty years ago.

For someone with the knowledge you are gaining right now, a mortgage may be considered as good debt because a properly structured mortgage isn't a simple debt, it is just the portion of the value of a durable asset in the *liabilities* column of your net worth calculation. Remember that your net worth is the sum of your assets minus liabilities. Real estate generally retains or gains value over long time periods so a mortgage can be arranged to ensure you always have some positive equity even if housing prices fluctuate. In this case, the asset value will always be greater than the liability in your net worth calculation.

Structuring such a mortgage usually means a down payment of 20% or more. The idea is that you own outright the equity portion of your house, and that equity can grow over time due to two factors: 1) asset appreciation, and 2) paydown of principle. Also, a mortgage is about the cheapest means of borrowing money you will ever find because the risk to the lender is minimal if you have made a good-sized down payment.

The total value of your house, not just your equity portion, fluctuates along with the housing market in your area. That's a form of leveraging money in a real estate investment, and the risks are very low as long as you have adequate income to make the mortgage payments. Any funds you would otherwise have used to pay down your mortgage faster than required can be put into alternative investments, and now those funds can earn money for you at the same time. The net result is two simultaneously appreciating assets: the equity in your real estate, and your investment portfolio. If structured safely in this way, mortgage debt can definitely be a wealth-building opportunity.

Let's look at a quick and easy example to see how much this good debt could be worth in terms of asset appreciation. If you bought a $500K house with a 20% down payment, plus 5% closing costs, you would have to come up with an investment of $125K and acquire a mortgage, or "good debt", of $400k. The costs of interest payments on your mortgage, insurance, property taxes, utilities, and maintenance would be similar to what you would otherwise pay for renting a place to live, so they can be excluded from this rough calculation. If the real estate value increased over the long term at about 5.5% annually (which American residential real estate has historically done, on average, over the last 60+ years) your $125K investment could turn into a $2.5 million real estate asset after the 30-year term of your mortgage. Your return on investment (ROI) would therefore be 2000% over that time span, or a 10.5% compound annual growth rate (CAGR). Your real estate investment (the $125K) would grow much faster than the real estate value itself precisely *because* you had good debt (your mortgage) leveraging your down payment. You only invest $125K but you experience the growth of a $500K asset.

Bad debt is tied to depreciating assets, like car loans. These debts should be avoided if at all possible; and if they are unavoidable, they should be paid off as quickly as possible. Car payments rob you of funds that could otherwise be working for you. With a car loan, or debt on any other depreciating asset, at least there is the possibility of selling the item and paying off the debt, but with depreciating assets, it's very easy to owe more than the item is worth. It is therefore paramount that you aggressively avoid debt on assets of this type. A more thorough analysis of just how great an opportunity exists for those who avoid this kind of bad debt will be presented shortly. (Note: this isn't the normal definition of bad debt, which is simply the status of a loan where the borrower cannot pay it back or even make interest payments. That is *bad* debt all right, but it's not the sense in which we are using the term here. We are just contrasting bad debt for depreciating assets vs. good debt that is inexpensive, low risk, and tied to an appreciating asset.)

Lastly, let's look at ugly debt. This is where there is no asset at all associated with the payments that must be made. You should keenly avoid debts of this nature if at all possible. If you already have ugly debt, use all the income-generating and cost-cutting principles taught throughout this book to find ways to get rid of it ASAP before you even begin to get money working for you. Examples of ugly debt are credit card debt (which is any amount you can't completely pay off with every monthly statement), personal loans (where there is no underlying asset tied to the payments), unpaid taxes (which is any amount owed to the IRS or any municipal, state, or federal government agency), and worst of all, anything like debt to family members, friends or gambling debts. If you have any ugly debts, you already know what they are so you must take immediate action to eradicate them and commit to never going into debt of this kind again. Don't take offense if you absolutely need a short-term loan from a family member or friend to get through some dire situation, but be sure to pay it off completely before you start investing. Relationships could be destroyed if a person you owe money to finds out you have investments.

Mathematically it is clear that paying off personal loans and credit card debt should be done before putting money to work on behalf of your family. Psychologically, however, a case could be made for starting to invest even while you have unpaid bad debt. The reason is that unpaid debt could be used as an excuse to postpone initiating the *Newborn Nest Egg* formula. At a later time, presumably when you are out of debt, you may forget, or be less inspired to take action, and the formula might never get implemented, thereby foregoing millions of dollars over the lifetime of your family. Also, setting up an obligation to an automated investment system may inspire you to get that bad debt paid off more quickly. Only you can make this judgment call, so do it prudently – no blaming and no complaining!

Just to wrap up this debt topic, there is one type of debt that falls outside all these categories, and that's student loan debt. This debt is hopefully associated with an underlying asset, and it does have monetary value; it's your education. This is an asset because you should be able to sell it in the form of a higher-paying job; presumably your education will make your services more valuable. But you won't instantly recover the costs you incurred to earn that education, and you certainly can't sell your degree to someone else and use the proceeds to pay off your student loan. If you and/or your spouse still have student debt at this stage of your life, calculate the interest rate on the loans and compare it to what you could be making in investments. The interest rate on most student loans is fairly low. If your investment returns are safe and substantially higher than the interest rate on the debt, it's OK to pay off any student loans slowly and invest as much as possible instead. Also, once the student loans are paid off there should be additional funds at the bottom line of your budget that could be used to increase your wealth more rapidly.

It is critical to understand that just avoiding debt is only half the battle. The true benefit is only realized when you invest the amount you would otherwise have wasted paying interest on bad or ugly debt. The difference between interest paid and interest earned is what is truly shocking, as you will see shortly. Now let's look at some ways to increase the bottom line of your budget so that you can get more money working for you. Increases can be generated by both cost-cutting and added income, and you are about to see some surprisingly simple yet powerful approaches that can produce incredible results.

Asset Classes & Opportunity Cost

To understand the vast difference between appreciating assets and depreciating assets we will use the two most common examples that almost everyone has some experience with, either first-hand or from family and friends. The obvious example of a depreciating asset is a vehicle, and of an appreciating asset is a house. This topic is specifically about growing your own nest egg, as distinct from your children's, but the principles apply directly to finding tradeoffs in your budget that increase your bottom line to generate a safety nest.

Let's start with the bad news, from the financial perspective, which is owning a vehicle, and show that it can represent a huge opportunity. Some people simply must have a vehicle for their lifestyle, and others just love cars. I have to admit that for me it's always been a bit of both. The important thing is to realize just how drastically the full cost of vehicle ownership can deteriorate your foundational wealth, and hence your ability to grow a nest egg. The silver lining in this situation, however, is just how enormous an opportunity it represents, as you'll soon see. We'll use an example to illustrate the point.

If you were to buy a new vehicle for $50,000 plus tax, you could get a decent quality vehicle of almost any model that suits your lifestyle, but nothing extravagant. In fact, this is the Kelley Blue Book average cost of a new car in America today. Let's assume this is your choice but you don't have the funds to buy it in cash, so you finance the purchase at a 5% annualized rate over a five-year term. In this situation, let's determine the full costs of vehicle ownership over the first five years, and then the second five-year period (don't worry if you don't want to concentrate enough to carefully follow this math, it's only the end results that must be understood).

Your initial down payment on a $50,000 vehicle will be about 20%, so that's $10,000. Then tax will be added, which averages 6% across all States, so there's another $3,000. Your monthly payments will be $755 per month, and included in that will be interest payments that add up to $5,300. Over the first five-year term, your vehicle costs will therefore be $50,000 (price) + $3,000 (tax) + $5,300 (interest) = $58,300. During those first five years, the vehicle will have dropped to half its original value so the residual value of this car at the five-year mark will be about $25,000 according to Kelly Blue Book. Your financial losses so far will therefore be $33,300. Assuming the monthly payments go away after five years, and that during the second five years the vehicle will only depreciate by another 1/2 of its residual value, your additional losses will be another $12,500. The net result in this example is that you spent $58,300, and ten years later you have a car that's worth $12,500, so you have lost $45,800, which averages $4,580 per year.

That's a significant amount in most family budgets but it's just the tip of the iceberg because it's nowhere near the total cost of owning and operating this vehicle. Every year, insurance averages $2,500, gas averages $5,000, maintenance averages $800, and repairs average $650. Over the first five years, this adds another $8,300 per year (assuming repairs are covered under warranty - although cosmetic and accidental mechanical damage are not). Over the next five years the combined extra costs average $8,950 per year. Parking is additional, and can be very significant if the car is used for commuting to work and your employer doesn't provide free parking. Clearly it is less expensive to keep a car for ten years or longer, but during those first ten years, a $50,000 vehicle will actually cost you about $132,000 when operating costs are included.

If you must have a vehicle, you can avoid some of the expense by simply buying it used, for cash. Five years old is approximately the sweet spot because a lot of vehicles are still perfectly good at this age, and the majority of their depreciation has already been absorbed by someone else. The risk of major repair bills, however, now falls to your account because the warranty typically expires by this time. Besides the usual tires, brakes, and battery, which will inevitably need to be replaced, a motor overhaul costs about $5,000, and transmission about $4,000 (this is just for average commuter cars, nothing like a pickup truck, large SUV, or luxury car). If you buy an EV, especially a used one, and need to replace the battery pack, you're looking at $10,000 to $20,000, and this expense will be incurred every 10 to 20 years, or 100,000 to 200,000 miles. These expenses aren't necessarily expected so we won't even include them in our total cost of ownership calculations. Just recognize that, as drastic a burden on your budget as vehicle ownership can be, it could prove to be even worse if any of these major expenses show up.

I learned this lesson the hard way a number of years ago when I thought I had reached a point in my life where my family deserved a luxury sport sedan. I had some money by then and foolishly thought I should be driving the type of car I could afford. Because I am of

German descent, and an engineer, I only considered German-engineered automobiles. I settled on a V8-powered 5-series BMW. The thing with this higher-end car was that everything about owning and operating it cost a lot more than for ordinary cars: it required premium gas – and consumed a lot of it; insurance was much more expensive; tires wore out faster because of the extra traction they provided; tires also cost a lot more because they were very wide, low profile, and high-speed rated; every battery replacement cost over $1,000; brakes wore out faster and cost a lot more than those of a regular car; even an oil change service was about four times as much as for other cars. And worst of all, that car was too smart for its own good; the sensors and control modules were extremely sensitive to any perceived anomaly. The BMW service manager told me it had like 4,000 sensors, so most of the faults it detected were just due to malfunctioning sensors.

As you can see, the cost of vehicle ownership is very high, and the majority comes from operating costs and the hidden cost of depreciation. There is another major factor to be considered, however, which most people see as devastating but we will think of as the silver lining. It is known as opportunity cost, and it is greater than all the other costs combined. It is called a cost because it refers to the financial gains you could otherwise have made by putting the same amount of money into investments instead of spending it on a depreciating vehicle with high operating costs. For our purposes, let's just call it *opportunity* because it's a single lifestyle choice you can make that could provide an entire nest egg! I'll demonstrate the math, but again, don't worry too much if you don't follow every step, it's the end result that is shocking.

In our example of the new, $50,000 vehicle, we determined it would cost $132,000 to own and operate for ten years. What financial opportunity could be gained by finding a way to avoid making this purchase?

Even if we just take the $132,000 and divide it equally between the ten years (which is more conservative than the actual purchase because the down payment and taxes are paid up-front), that's $13,200 per year, or $1,100 per month. A 10-year investment of $1,100 per month, growing at an annual rate of 10% on average, produces a return on investment of about $99,000. The total costs of owning and operating that $50,000 car, including opportunity cost, are therefore more like $231,000 over ten years. This means that if you could live without that new car, and committed to putting the equivalent amounts into your investment account instead, 10 years later you could have an extra $231,000 working for you.

But we're not nearly done yet! If, at that point, you made no additional investment, just foregoing this one vehicle purchase and choosing to invest the funds instead, should now be earning you an extra $23,000 per year. That sounds pretty good, but how is this for shock and awe: If that $231,000 were left to compound for the subsequent 30 years at 10% CAGR it would become over $4 million! And if you kept contributing the equivalent costs of owning and operating an average new car every ten years, estimated at $13,200 per year, your portfolio value after 40 years (assuming age 25 to 65) would be over $6.4 million! This doesn't even include the inflation factors that would inevitably make the alternative use of these funds increase dramatically over that 40-year timespan (the vehicle purchases and operating expenses), all of which could be avoided if you didn't own those vehicles.

FINANCIAL FACTOR	COST	% OF 10-YR COST	COMMENT
FINANCING	$5,300	3.9%	Often feared as a large % of cost
TAX AND DEPRECIATION	$45,800	33.4%	Financial losses due to ownership – about ½ as significant as operating costs
OPERATING	$86,200	62.7%	The greatest cost besides opportunity
OPPORTNITY (10-YEAR)	$231,000		By far the greatest financial factor
1ST CAR OPPORTUNITY (40-YEAR)	$4,000,000		Generated by foregoing your first new car and investing the savings for 40 years
4-CAR OPPORTUITY (40-YEAR)	$6,400,000		Generated by foregoing an average new car every 10 years and investing the savings

Analysis of Vehicle Cost Factors

The question you have to ask yourself is this, would you rather own an average new car every ten years or have $6.4 million extra in retirement?

The lesson I finally learned from owning the BMW was that, while I loved driving that car, I did not enjoy owning it. It was not until I looked back on that experience and did the above calculations that I realized my total cost of ownership for that car. Comparing my experience to the example I presented of the average cost of vehicle ownership, my costs were more than double. Once I realized how much wealth-building opportunity I had given up by owning that car (and the various other expensive cars, trucks, and SUVs I had owned) I finally began to drive inexpensive vehicles regardless of what I could afford. And yes, I invest the difference.

The point is that owning and operating vehicles is full of hidden costs and opportunity costs that will never be shown in the flashy commercials. Eliminating them is therefore one of the greatest strategies for increasing your foundational wealth, and it is a *massive* increase!

This one lifestyle choice could completely pay for a lavish retirement. Of course, it only works in your favor if you actually invest the amounts you would otherwise have spent to own and operate new vehicles.

I have dedicated considerable space in this book to this one subject, but for good reason. If your income situation makes it difficult to cut costs and set aside funds to invest, this one move could be a solution for you. It may not be easy but it's worth so much that strong consideration should be given to finding a way. As you are about to see, your vehicle ownership decisions can be about as lucrative as owning a house. If your financial situation makes home ownership unattainable, eliminating vehicle ownership, and investing the cost-savings, could be an equally powerful way of generating a nest egg.

This opportunity is so valuable that if your residence location in relation to your place of employment isn't conducive to living without a vehicle, you could consider changing jobs or moving closer to your job. You may believe there is some social stigma attached to riding public transit to work, but that sensation can be more than offset by the knowledge that your strategy will net millions of dollars in value over the span of your career. And heck, once you've got millions of dollars working for you, go ahead and buy a really nice car if you want to.

Clearly, eliminating vehicle ownership is not an option for everyone, and it's not that giving up on owning cars is absolutely necessary. The important thing to understand is just how much wealth-building opportunity you could otherwise take advantage of before you decide which path is more beneficial. The above calculations clearly demonstrate that if you do own a vehicle, most of the opportunity lies in eliminating the depreciation and operating costs over decades. If you must own a vehicle, or vehicles, find ways to mitigate these costs, invest the savings, and you will do well financially.

Also note that vehicle ownership is just one example of an expense that incurs opportunity cost. Anything you are considering spending money on that is not an investment should be analyzed for its full cost including depreciation and opportunity cost. You now know how to calculate the future value of investing the funds you are considering spending on things like an RV/camping trailer, boat, motorcycle, vacations, furniture, appliances, entertainment systems, jewelry, or status symbols of any kind.

Now let's take a more detailed look at our chosen example of an appreciating asset: buying a house. We will refer to residential real estate as an appreciating asset because, as pointed out earlier, this asset class has historically gained value over long timeframes, and the *Newborn Nest Egg* formula is only appropriate for long-term investing. Let's go through a hypothetical example to demonstrate how this could work in your favor.

The average price of a single-family dwelling in the US at the time of this writing is $420,000, so we'll use that as our proposed purchase price. If this price would not even buy a 1-bedroom apartment where you live, stick with me as this is just an example. There are a number of fees involved in a real estate transaction, and we won't get into the details, but they can be summarized as *closing costs*, and they typically add up to about 5%. In most cases, unfortunately, these additional fees can't be factored into the mortgage, they must be paid by the purchaser at the time of the transaction. In the case of our example $420,000 house, this adds $21,000.

The other major expense is the down payment. A 20% down payment is required by most banks or mortgage providers in order to keep their risks low. An alternative is to buy mortgage insurance, in which case a mortgage might be available with as little as a 5% down payment. This mortgage insurance has an additional monthly fee, of course, plus the mortgage is for a greater amount, so monthly mortgage costs will also be higher. In our example, let's keep it simple and assume you can come up with a 20% down payment, plus the closing costs. For our hypothetical $420,000 house this means a down payment of $84,000 plus $21,000 in closing costs, for a total cash investment of $105,000 and a mortgage of $336,000.

Notice that a house purchase is literally an investment because the money is not gone, it has just been converted from cash into home equity, which will typically increase in value as enough time goes by, so it is actually a real estate investment. Now let's look at how well this investment should perform over the long term. Gains will be made on the full value of the property, not just on the $105,000 invested, so with our historical average of 5.5% annualized growth rate, the property value will increase from $420,000 to $3.6 million in 40 years (assuming age 25 to 65 again for the owner). Don't get too excited quite yet because we still have to count the costs. Additional expenses that would not apply if you did not own a home include: mortgage interest, property taxes, insurance, utilities, maintenance, and repairs. If you didn't purchase a house, however, there would be offsetting alternative costs such as rent, utilities, and insurance, and all of these would increase at least at the rate of inflation, so the costs of homeownership are still a much better option. The even better news is that mortgages can typically be locked in for 30 years at a fixed rate if you have made the 20% down payment (in the US), so these fees are not affected by inflation the way rent would be. If you happen to buy a house when interest rates are high, you can always refinance your mortgage when rates drop, then keep it locked in at the lower rate. In addition, in many circumstances, the interest paid on the mortgage for a primary residence is tax deductible in the US. We won't calculate that benefit, but it only adds to your return on investment.

Without bogging down in the details let's cut to the chase. 30-year Mortgage rates have averaged about 4% over the past fifteen years or more, so that's a reasonable long-term assumption. The monthly mortgage cost for our example house purchase will therefore be about $1600, for a total of $577,000 over 30 years. That will pay off the mortgage principal of $336,000 plus the interest costs of $241,000. The additional costs of property taxes and homeowner's insurance will add another $450 per month, so that's another $162,000. Adjusted for inflation, this will end up being more like $500,000 over 40 years. The remaining costs of home ownership such as utilities and maintenance would be approximately offset by similar costs if you were renting, so we'll ignore them. The bottom line then is that buying this house will likely result in a gain of: $3.6 million (property value) - $105,000 (down payment and closing costs) -$241,000 (mortgage interest) - $500,000 (property taxes and insurance) = $2.8 million net gain.

It should be blindingly obvious by now that investing in appreciating assets, especially a house, is vastly superior to buying depreciating assets like vehicles. In our examples, both spanning 40 years, buying an average new car every ten years would incur a net cost (including operating costs, depreciation, and financial loss of opportunity) of $6.4 million, while the purchase of an average house can produce a net gain of $2.8 million.

> **This bears repeating. If you forego buying an average new car every ten years, but you do buy a house, the difference to your net worth at retirement age could be in the range of $9.2 million!**

But wait, there's more! There is another great potential benefit to owning a house – you can generate almost passive income with it by renting out a secondary suite, or two, either long-term or Airbnb-style. This extra income can offset your mortgage payments and thereby increase your investments elsewhere. Without doing a whole analysis, suffice it to say that renting out a secondary suite or suites can earn you the equivalent of 75% to 100% of your mortgage costs, or more. For example, if you were to rent out a secondary suite in your house, or operate it as an Airbnb, generating perhaps an extra $1,000 per month, then invest that income at 10% annually, this would add *another* $5.8 million to your net worth after 40 years.

> **Yes, you read that correctly: investing the income from renting out a secondary suite can generate substantially more net worth than the appreciating value of the house itself!**

An even more lucrative strategy to consider as young parents is to buy your first home with the right location, layout, size, and features to be used as a rental property five to ten years down the road. This kind of house may not be your ideal long-term home but if it's suitable for renting, maybe as two separate units (upstairs and downstairs, for instance), it might be an ideal starter home. When you can afford a better home, keep the starter home as a rental property and move into something better. If your second home also contains a secondary suite, you've got potentially three rental incomes. That goes a long way towards paying mortgages and building your nest egg investments.

Owning a house, or houses, can therefore be understood as part of your own retirement nest egg. It's a relatively safe, long-term-growth asset, and it can generate additional income. A perfectly reasonable retirement nest egg strategy for yourselves as new parents might be to avoid buying a new car (maybe get by with one used car instead of two new ones), buy a house as soon as possible, rent out a secondary suite, and put those cost-savings and extra income into the same investments you will be learning about shortly as your *Newborn Nest Egg* formula. This real estate investment, plus the nest egg investment, plus your 401(k), IRA, and any other pension, should generate plenty of net worth during your career to fund a very comfortable and early retirement. And along the way, it won't cost a noticeable amount in terms of restricting any of your other lifestyle choices. You will live just as comfortably as you would if you owned that extra new car and didn't rent out a secondary suite in your house. In a sense, these strategies create almost free money – lots of it! And once you have enough money working for you, the passive income literally becomes a cash cow (OK, cash cow isn't literal, but you understand the metaphor). This can lead to an early, luxurious, retirement while providing generational wealth for your family.

A colleague I worked with followed this strategy. He was a single guy who drove an inexpensive used car and owned a medium-sized, two-bedroom condo close to where we worked. He rented out one bedroom to a roommate and occupied the other one himself. He also bought a house in a rural area where costs were lower. He rented the upper floor of that house to one family and the lower level to another couple. This house was too far from our office for him to live there and commute to work, but close enough that he could easily access it as necessary for maintenance, repairs, or tenant turnover. His relatively simple real estate arrangements generated considerable wealth because both his own accommodation and his rental house were generating positive cash flow, decreasing mortgage costs, and vastly increasing asset values. That's a win, win, win! I have no doubt that he owns additional rental properties by now, has a very substantial investment portfolio, or both. Either way, he has ample, growing wealth, and significant passive income.

CHAPTER 4

SYNDICATES AND SECURITIES

What I Wish I had Known

My wife and I have a daughter and a son who are very close in age. We started saving and investing for their college education from birth. Early in their middle school years, I began to recognize the challenges they would be facing when starting their careers. All their college funds would be gone, and despite our planning ahead, they were still likely to have negative net worth as they entered adulthood. To counteract this, I started an investment fund for each of them and managed it using the same strategy I used for my own investments at that time.

I had previously used stock brokers and wealth managers, and had followed their advice for investment in mutual funds and a few individual stock picks. My results had been abysmal. At the point where I began investing on behalf of our kids, I had just switched to online, self-directed brokerage accounts, and was attempting to follow the advice of several investment-advisory subscriptions. These services were advertised with pitch points such as, "You could have made gains like 151% if you'd followed my recommendations on _ _ _ Corp. or a phenomenal 436% from my advice on _ _ _". It all sounded so convincing, and I was determined to make it work for my family.

It did not work! And worse than that, it consumed the majority of my parenting time. Most days I would come home from work, have dinner with my family, then spend the evening in my home office "doing investing". The process wasn't making anywhere near the gains of the few hand-picked examples that had been used in the marketing pitch. It was also robbing me of spending time with my kids, which was much more important than a bit more money for their future. My biggest problem was that I wanted both, a solid financial foundation *and* quality time with my family, but I was accomplishing *neither*.

Up to that point, I simply didn't know how to achieve it; I didn't have the investing acumen to filter out all the rubbish and implement a successful set-and-forget program. Fortunately, by then my career had progressed into executive positions in public companies and I began to understand in great detail how stock markets and investing worked. That's when the *Newborn Nest Egg* formula began to take shape. I dropped all the time-consuming analysis, implementation, and monitoring of individual investment decisions and began studying how to invest passively on behalf of my family.

This chapter will provide the background necessary to understand simplified investing in the stock market. Following the *Newborn Nest Egg* formula does require you to become an investor, but don't let that scare you, intimidate you, or deter you. The information presented here is simple enough that you can easily follow it if you put in a little effort, and it's powerful enough that your financial gains will be as good as virtually any other investor. Comprehending the remainder of this book will make you a wise investor, confident enough that hearing about other strategies, no matter how attractive they may sound, will not make you question *your* strategy. The chapter starts out by describing how companies get to the stock market, and then explains why and how individuals can buy and sell shares of those companies. It is not necessary to understand all these details thoroughly in order to safely and successfully use the *Newborn Nest Egg* formula. The information is presented so that the step-by-step instructions to come will be unambiguous and precise, and so that readers will have confidence they are making sound investment decisions based on rigorous analysis. Without some solid fundamentals, you could easily be swayed by alternate strategies that can often sound much more exciting.

For most investors, particularly those just starting out, the best place to invest for passive financial gains is in the stock market. It allows you to start with virtually any amount of money (even zero dollars), can be done with very little time, effort, or stress, and it can build foundational wealth that underpins any other ventures you or your family decide to pursue. Of course, many undesirable outcomes are possible as well so it is critical to understand the right way to do it wisely. Any kind of investing can be a risky undertaking if attempted without a proven strategy, and the stock market is no exception. You may feel you are already familiar with how stock markets work but I predict that this section will provide at least a few new insights. For those who want to understand the fundamentals, or require a brief refresher, all the definitions and basic structures you need to know will be provided. Don't worry, you won't require in-depth comprehension of any advanced securities trading strategies or ongoing advisory services to follow the *Newborn Nest Egg* formula. It is important however to at least understand the concepts and terms used to discuss stock market investing, both in this book and with like-minded friends and colleagues.

Securities, Exchanges, and Indices

When we talk about investing in stocks and bonds, which are collectively referred to as securities, we need a certain amount of knowledge so we can understand and participate in financial conversations. Stocks are known as equity investments, because a stockholder, also known as a shareholder, owns a piece of the overall company; ownership equals equity. Bonds, on the other hand, are called debt investments, debt instruments, or fixed income securities, because they are a loan from the investor that puts the borrower into a bond, or contract, of debt to the lender. The borrower then pays a regular, fixed interest rate to the lender for the duration of the loan, and pays back the full value of the bond at the end of the contract. The total of all your combined investments in securities is called your investment portfolio.

All corporations start out as private companies. Some private companies, at a certain stage of their growth, decide to become public companies. The fundamental difference between a private company and a public company is its ability to sell shares to people who are not directly associated with the company, in other words, the general public. Many companies want the ability to sell shares to a multitude of shareholders so that they can raise a great deal of capital (money) in order to expand, grow, and become one of the dominant players in their industry. Another reason they go public is so that early investors, such as the founders and venture capital groups, have a way to pull some of their cash out of the company so they can invest it in other businesses at earlier stages of development. Pulling cash out means selling their shares to others, and the ability to sell to anyone through a public market is the best way to enable that.

A private company typically becomes a public company by offering to sell a portion of its shares to the public in what is called an Initial Public Offering (IPO). In order to begin selling shares to the general public, a company must meet all the requirements and criteria of whatever stock exchange they wish to have their shares trading on, all of which are regulated by the Securities and Exchange Commission (SEC). (This assumes an American procedure; other countries have similar corporate structures, stock exchanges, and regulatory bodies.) All public companies must have their shares listed for sale on one of the approved stock exchanges. These exchanges provide a way for anyone to buy or sell shares of any of their listed public companies on any business day. There are well over 5,000 public companies trading shares on the major stock exchanges in the US at this time.

The main stock exchanges in America are the New York Stock Exchange (NYSE), and the National Association of Securities Dealers Automated Quotations (NASDAQ). There are other exchanges for smaller companies, for commodities, and for currencies, but we won't get into those here. When shares of companies are listed for sale on a stock exchange, these shares are often referred to as stocks. When you buy or sell stock in a company you are "trading" shares of fractional ownership in that company for dollars. Each company's shares that trade on a stock exchange is identified with a unique trading symbol, also called a ticker symbol, or ticker. Here are some well-known trading symbols of prominent companies: **MSFT:** Microsoft Corporation; **AAPL:** Apple Inc.; **GOOGL:** Alphabet Inc. (Google); **AMZN:** Amazon.com Inc.; **FB:** Meta Platforms, Inc. (formerly Facebook); **TSLA:** Tesla, Inc.; **NVDA**: NVIDIA Corp; **NFLX:** Netflix, Inc.; **KO:** The Coca-Cola Company; **INTC:** Intel Corporation.

Next let's look at a brief overview of stock indexes, or indices. The most famous ones are the Dow Jones Industrial Average and the Stand & Poor's 500 Composite Index, often abbreviated as *the Dow* and *the S&P 500*. These indexes are just lists of companies that, in aggregate, provide a representation of what's going on in the stock markets as a whole. They are called stock indexes because the performance of the companies on these lists indicates what most investors are buying and selling by tracking the average price or value of selected subsets of public companies.

The Dow Index is a list of just 30 companies, typically the largest 30 public industrial corporations in America. The member companies that make up the Dow change from time to time, but the same 30 largest companies typically remain the largest for years. All 30 member companies that make up the Dow Index trade on either the NYSE or the NASDAQ. When the Dow goes up, it is an indication that the largest, most stable companies in the country (sometimes referred to as *blue-chip* stocks), are perceived by investors to be worth more than they were previously. Investors are voting with their wallets by buying these companies' shares for higher prices. This can be taken to mean that investors are generally feeling positive (bullish) about the economy of the country.

The S&P 500 is sometimes called the *broader market*. That's because this stock index looks at the average value of 500 large public companies. The selection criteria for being included in the Dow Index are slightly different than the criteria for being an S&P 500 component company. For this reason, there is not necessarily a complete overlap, however most, if not all, of the 30 companies that make up the Dow Jones Industrial Average are also included in the 500 companies that make up the S&P 500 Index.

In addition to trading individual stocks, it is possible to buy and sell shares of whole groups of companies simultaneously, up to and including all the companies that make up an entire stock index such as the Dow or the S&P 500. This is done by trading shares in what is called an exchange-traded fund (ETF). There are ETFs for all kinds of special interest investments such as groups of Tech companies, Bond companies, Gold companies, Financial companies, Real Estate companies, Growth companies, Emerging Market companies, Industrial companies, Cryptocurrencies, and entire market indices.

I am sometimes asked why we can't just invest in the Dow or the S&P 500, and the answer may not be as straightforward as you expect. The simple answer is that these are indices, which are just lists, not stocks or securities of any kind. The S&P 500, for example, is a list that is selected, organized, and presented using expert knowledge (i.e., curated) by a company called Standard & Poor's, but it is not a standalone public company. It is a division of S&P Global Inc., which is a public company. S&P Global Inc. is listed on the New York Stock Exchange under the ticker symbol **SPGI,** and it provides financial information and analytics, including credit ratings, indices (such as the S&P 500), and other financial data. **SPGI** is an S&P 500 component company, meaning it is one of the 500 leading public corporations trading on

American stock exchanges. We *could* just buy shares of **SPGI** but that would not be a diversified portfolio at all, it would simply be an investment in a single financial data company. It has no ownership nor control over the 500 companies it selects for its list which is called the S&P 500 Index.

To buy shares of the whole broader market simultaneously, which is what people probably mean when they want to invest in the S&P 500, we would have to buy shares of one of the S&P 500 ETFs (there are several of these to choose from). Each share of an S&P 500 ETF gets us a small portion of ownership in *all* the companies that make up the S&P 500 stock index, so it is an investment in a single ticker that provides vast diversity. The way this works is that a pool of money is collected from a bunch of individual investors, corporate investors, and institutional investors, by selling them shares of the ETF. The company that manages the ETF then invests this pool of money so that it owns shares of the same companies, in the same ratio, as those that make up the S&P 500 Index. The value of each of these ETFs will therefore grow and fluctuate at the same rate as the underlying group of companies, which is the same growth rate as the S&P 500 Index itself.

ETFs must be distinguished from mutual funds. They can easily be confused because they have some similarities, but the operating principles are completely different. An ETF simply identifies a segment of the market, or an entire stock index, and holds shares of the same companies, in the same ratios, as those that trade on the stock exchange. For instance, an S&P 500 ETF holds shares of *every* company in the so-called broader market. A tech ETF would hold only the shares of a selected group of tech companies that trade on the NASDAQ. In every ETF, the mix of companies and ratios of each would only change when the curator of the index makes changes to its list of member companies. This means that for the S&P 500, Standard & Poor's exclusively decides which companies make up its S&P 500 Composite Index.

A mutual fund also holds a bunch of different stocks, all focused on one market segment as per their stated investment focus, however, the individual stocks, the mix of stocks, and the weighting ratios will change all the time based on decisions of the mutual fund's management team. The net difference between the two structures is that an ETF requires essentially no ongoing management, because it can be automated, whereas a mutual fund requires continuous and intensive management scrutiny and stock trades. The cost to the investor is therefore vastly different as well. An ETF has no marketing or sales costs, exceedingly low annual management fees, and no front-end or back-end loads (all these fees are explained in Appendix A). Mutual funds unfortunately incur all the above fees, which are paid by you if you invest in them. The difference in structure between an ETF and a mutual fund makes them appropriate for different investment terms. A mutual fund may be less volatile and therefore safer for short-term investments, whereas ETFs will almost certainly provide superior gains over longer terms because their management fees are *much* lower. An example of comparative performance is provided in Appendix A.

The Wealth Management Industry

As mentioned previously, the wealth management and financial planning industry has been created as a way to profit from the lack of financial training provided to the rest of us in most of our schooling.

The industry is made up of a hierarchy of corporations employing specialists who have focused on studying business, accounting, banking, economics, or finance of some sort. As you can well imagine, none of these professionals work for free, nor should they. What this means is that if you can do things for yourself, you can save all the costs that the numerous, highly paid employees of this industry must charge for their services. And as you'll soon see, these savings can be substantial.

To understand just how much money is involved in providing financial planning services to individuals (referred to as retail investors) it is necessary to understand the components of the industry and the hierarchy. Don't worry too much about remembering all of this because it's not the details that matter, it's the fact that there is so much money involved, which means there is so much opportunity available to you. I will therefore keep the details brief, but again, a *Newborn Nest Egg* investor would want to know what's going on behind the scenes.

We will start with an explanation of the bottom layer of the industry, then look at the hierarchy above it. Let's say that around the time you are starting your family, you see a poster in your bank proclaiming that they can help guide your investing decisions and ensure that you reach your financial goals. This sounds good to you because you are young, beginning to earn an adequate income, and are aware that starting to invest early in life is a smart move. You go ahead and make an appointment to meet with someone on the 16th to discuss what the bank can do for you in this regard. The person you meet with has a nice office behind the scenes from all the hubbub of tellers and ATM kiosks. She has a couple of framed diplomas on her office wall making it clear to you that she has a university degree and a designation as a Certified Financial Planner. Predictably, she looks into your accounts, gathers as much information from you as possible about your income and expenses, your current financial condition (assets and liabilities), calculates from that what your "net worth" is, and asks about your financial goals, risk tolerance, and other life ambitions. From all this data, you jointly determine with her how much money you have to invest right now, and how much you are willing to add to your investments every month. That concludes the first meeting, and she promises that within a week or so you will receive a documented financial plan tailored specifically to your situation. When this plan is ready, you meet with her again to review it. It demonstrates in colorful detail how you will make modest but steady gains in a balanced portfolio of mutual funds, as long as you diligently stick to the plan, and nothing much ever changes in your life. Every chart is trending steadily but modestly up and to the right for the rest of your life. It demonstrates that you may be able to reach some of your financial and other life goals as long as you don't aim for anything very lofty.

This scenario represents the bottom level of the financial planning industry, meaning it is the level that interacts with retail investors like the majority of personal banking customers. The written plan produced by the financial planner will undoubtedly recommend a balanced and diversified portfolio. To accomplish this with relatively small initial investment resources, the majority of the plan will be to buy units of mutual funds. The recommended mutual funds will be primarily made up of growth stocks, because you, as a young adult, can withstand some risk and volatility in exchange for higher growth potential. For diversity, some of the recommended mutual funds will focus on technology companies while others will focus on things like financial services, medical services, and pharmaceuticals that are generally more stable. There will likely also be an international fund that focuses on "emerging markets" because the really big gains can be made in countries that are just entering the worldwide economy, and they may have abundant natural resources or cheap labor. There will be at least one or two bond funds in the mix as well to balance your portfolio and thereby reduce your volatility and overall risk.

What are these mutual funds, and how do they come to be the cornerstone of a retail investor's financial plan? Great question; and seeking the answer will guide us through the hierarchy of the financial planning and wealth management industry. As an aside, when a person has significant amounts of money to invest, they don't call it financial planning any more, they prefer to call it *wealth management*. It is supposed to make the client feel like they have already achieved the accumulation of some wealth and now just need the professionals to step in and manage that wealth, so it doesn't get lost. At this higher level of investible resources, it is more feasible to have a person's portfolio made up of some hand-picked individual stocks and bonds, although mutual funds are generally still a significant part of the mix.

> **Mutual funds are the backbone of financial planning and wealth management because they are said to provide two key advantages: 1) They provide a much greater level of diversity than a small portfolio of individual stocks and/or bonds, and 2) The securities that make up the funds are selected and actively managed by specialists with a reputation for success.**

A mutual fund is a financial product, also known as an investment vehicle, that pools money from multiple sources to invest in a diversified portfolio of stocks, bonds, or other securities. This pooling of resources allows individual investors to participate in a diversified and professionally managed portfolio, even with relatively small amounts of their own money. There are four broad types of mutual funds: equity (stocks), fixed income (bonds), money market funds (short-term debt), or a mix of stocks and bonds (balanced or hybrid funds). The capital required to form a mutual fund comes from numerous sources such as retail investors, corporate pension funds, endowment funds of universities, charitable foundations, etc. This pool of capital is then invested in a number of individual securities such as stocks and bonds. The stock and/or bond picks, as well as the balancing of how much is invested in each, are made by a fund manager or management team. The entire fund is divided into units so that each unit represents ownership of a small fraction of the whole portfolio. In this way, the relatively small investment capital of an individual can afford the services of professional investment managers, and can benefit from the greater balance and diversity of a larger basket of securities. Sounds like a win-win, right?

Well, maybe. But the flip side of the coin is that there are a lot of fees being charged along the way because so many people need to get paid to support this infrastructure. It sounds efficient because a potentially huge pool of funds is managed by a very small team. The real cost, however, is in the layers of sales and marketing that go into selling these fund units to you, the retail investor. There are a lot of different mutual funds out there, and therefore a lot of competition to get retailers of financial products (banks, savings & loan companies, brokerage houses, financial planning firms, wealth management firms, insurance brokers, etc.) to sell units of a particular mutual fund or family of funds. Just like virtually every other product, the financial products that are recommended are not necessarily what's best for the consumer but what is most financially rewarding to the seller.

Most mutual funds come from organizations that are in the business of creating and selling large numbers of investment products. Each individual fund, or product, is therefore part of a conglomerate of such funds, all sold through the same channels, at least at the wholesale level. A fund is created by figuring out a catchy market segment to focus their investments on, and pairing this product with a manager or management team possessing the appropriate expertise. The organization then finds initial sources of investment capital from financial institutions and looks for additional money to manage by selling units of the fund. This process pools the investments of many individuals and organizations into a single pot of funds that is managed on behalf of all investors mutually, thus the term mutual fund.

Examples of mutual fund niches include Growth Funds, Value Funds, Blended Funds, Technology Sector Funds, Healthcare Sector Funds, Financial Sector Funds, International Funds, Emerging Market Funds, High-Yield Bond Funds, Commodity Funds, Dividend Growth Funds, and the list goes on and on. Once a new fund with some particular focus is established, it is typically packaged up with other mutual funds within the same organization and presented to distributors of such packages or families of funds. The packages that provide the best financial incentives to the distribution channels get brought into the mix of financial products they promote, and ultimately get sold down through the supply chain. The expensive incentives that are used to push families of funds through these channels include things like lavish conferences, dinners, rounds of golf, and even all-expense paid seminars at resorts. When the packages are sold, the business development managers and account managers are paid handsome commissions and bonuses. They often earn over $500,000 each per year in salary, commissions, and bonuses. Executives and fund managers earn even more.

And how do distributors of financial products bring their bundles of funds to market? Well, as you already suspect, they provide financial incentives for the wholesalers to sell their products. This is done by paying additional incentives, and by promoting their opportunities with another level of similar free perks. Successful sales at this level of the supply chain are also rewarded with lucrative commissions and bonuses paid to the sales and management professionals. Eventually these wholesalers present the products to the retail level representatives (financial planners at banks and the like) and provide them with their own set of perks and payments for selling the financial products through retailers. This structure encompasses many additional employees, each earning hundreds of thousands of dollars per year.

The dichotomy between investment recommendations to retail investors vs. the benefits they brought to the investment advisory industry got so bad in the US that in 2019, the Securities and Exchange Commission created what they called Regulation Best Interest (Reg BI), which requires broker-dealers to act in the best interest of their customers and mitigate conflicts of interest. This was by no means the first or only time the SEC had to slap the wrists of the financial planning industry for enriching themselves at the expense of their clients – and the trend continues.

If this seems inefficient and expensive, it is! But there is so much money to be made that almost everyone in the distribution channel gets paid generously. So where does all that money come from? That's the right question for a *Newborn Nest Egg* investor to ask. The name of the game in financial planning and wealth management is a key metric called Assets Under Management (AUM), and here's why it is so important and so lucrative for them. All the costs and expenses in the industry are paid for by charging clients an annual fee that is a percentage of the total value of their portfolios. Fees for retail investors range from about 2% to 1% of the individual's total portfolio value – every year! When portfolio values are pooled into massive funds, such as in mutual funds, or the aggregate of all portfolios in large wealth management firms, the dollar values get astronomical. A small wealth management firm, at the top level of the financial products hierarchy, might have $100 Billion worth of AUM. A large firm will have $trillions. Even just 1% of a trillion dollars is $10 Billion. That's ten billion dollars every year that can be used to pay professionals' salaries and all kinds of sales and marketing incentives, commissions, bonuses, and perks along the way.

But isn't 2% or 1% of an individual's total portfolio value a pretty insignificant amount? I have invested in mutual funds myself in the past, and thought it was an acceptable fee to pay for expertise I did not possess at the time. When you receive your financial plan from the representative at your bank, she will assure you that the professional investors who are now managing your funds will easily do 2% better than you would do on your own, so it's not really costing you anything. If you weren't a *Newborn Nest Egg* investor that might very well be true, but those days are soon to be over.

Let's have a look at the same numbers, but from a different perspective, with a hypothetical example. Let's say you have been saving and investing for a while and have built up a portfolio worth $100,000. The balanced and diversified funds your planner has you invested in may generate 6% compound annual growth rate (CAGR), but it is supposedly a stable and safe 6%. That's not too bad, right? It should double your money every 12 years or so. But now think about the cost of that 2% of portfolio value you pay out every year. That's 2% of $100,000, which is $2,000 every year, and it theoretically goes up as your portfolio gains value. Even just $2,000 per year for 12 years has cost you $24,000! 12 years from now it should be 2% of $200,000, so $4,000 per year (this doesn't even include the additional money you would add to your portfolio along the way). Without that 2% management fee, you would be earning 8% from the exact same investments. In that case you would be doubling your money every 9 years instead of 12. In terms of your gains, you are paying 2% to earn 6%, which would otherwise be 8%. That means you are giving up 25% of your gains. Remember how a dollar saved is two dollars earned? You would need a pay raise of $8000 per year just to cover the cost of that 2% management fee. And that's just at the $200,000 portfolio level. What happens when you hit a million?

The question you have to ask yourself is: are these mutual funds I'm being offered (which I now know are sold to me because they provide more financial incentives for everyone in the distribution chain rather than providing the best benefit to me), really earning me 25% better gains than I could make myself?

With this new insight into just how much of your gains are being paid for professional management of your portfolio, you rush back to the bank for another meeting with your financial planner. You explain why you think you are being charged too much. Then you add some new information you recently discovered, which is that others are paying only 1% of their portfolio value per year for the same services. You demand a reduced rate. "Oh, no sir", says your financial planning professional with a glance towards her framed diplomas, "those rates are reserved for our wealthy clients with over a million dollars in their portfolios. You're still a long way from reaching our elite status, but here is a free pen with our name and phone number on it. Call us any time you have extra money to invest."

CHAPTER 5

TO BUY OR NOT TO BUY

The Power of the Snowball Effect

The idea of investments having a snowball effect was made popular by the most successful investor of recent times, Warren Buffett (not to be confused with the late Jimmy Buffett who spent a lot more time in Margaritaville). To understand the basic principle of a snowball, don't think about the kind kids pack between their mittens and throw at each other. Think of the kind they roll across their front lawn to build a snowman. The basic idea is that the bigger the snowball gets, the faster it gets bigger. This image was Mr. Buffett's way of making the concept of passively growing wealth easy to understand and hard to forget.

> This is probably the most important concept in investing, which is the whole idea behind getting your money working for you instead of you

**working for your money. In finance-speak, this
snowball effect is known as compounding.**

In dollar terms, it is easiest to explain with a quick example. Let's say
you have $10,000 invested and it earns a 10% annualized return on
investment (ROI), also called a rate-of-return, or an annual growth
rate. After one year you will have 10% more, which is $1,000 more,
so your total at year-end will be $11,000. Assuming you keep all of
those funds invested at the same ROI, the following year you will have
$12,100. In the third year you will have $13,310 and so on. To verify
these calculations yourself, simply multiply the invested amount at the
beginning of each year by 1.1 (for our 10% growth rate example) to
determine the value at each year-end. When you let your investment
grow year after year without extracting or spending any of the change
in value, it produces a compounding return on investment, known as
a compound annual growth rate, or CAGR. This CAGR might be
positive or negative, depending on whether the underlying securities
increased or decreased in value, on average, during the specified time
period.

What you will find is that at a 10% CAGR, your investment doubles
every 7.2 years. This outcome has led to a term called "the rule of 72".
It's a way of quickly estimating in your head how long it will take to
double your money with any given rate of return. It works by dividing
72 by the CAGR to get the approximate number of years required
to double your money. In the example above, 72 divided by 10 (as in
10% compound annual growth rate) will get you the 7.2 years we just
calculated. If your annual rate of return was just 5%, 72 divided by 5
would estimate 14.4 years to double your money. No surprise there;
it takes twice as long at half the rate of return. Let's try a few other

estimates: 72/8 means it will take about 9 years to double your money at an 8% CAGR, and 72/12 means it will take just 6 years to double your money if you can generate a 12% compound annual growth rate.

Now think about how powerful this is. With $10,000 invested at 10% CAGR, your money can earn another $10,000 for you in 7.2 years. Then it can earn an additional $20,000 in the next 7.2 years, and grow by $40,000 more in the third 7.2-year period. That means you'll have $80,000 after 21.6 years, $160,000 after 28.8 years, and $320,000 after 36 years. Not bad for just a one-time $10,000 investment, but you can do better. The key takeaway here is to realize the enormous value of that one commodity your kids already have more of than almost anyone else on earth: time! 36 years could turn $10,000 into $320,000, and it happens without having to do anything but wait.

> **In this example, you worked to earn the initial $10,000, and then your money worked to earn you $310,000 more. In the 36-year period of this investment, your money earned 31 times as much as you did; and *time* was the most valuable factor!**

This is the essence of getting your money working for you, so you don't have to keep working for your money all your life. Investments can generate completely passive income, as long as they don't need to be actively managed, which is a key tenet of the *Newborn Nest Egg* formula.

In the real world of investing, of course, rates of return are not steady at all - they typically bounce up and down like a stair climber. For our purposes, we simply need to understand that rates of return on investments will always fluctuate but they can still be analyzed and even predicted to some extent. You will always see the disclaimer in any financial forecast that goes something like this: *past performance is not a reliable indicator of future success*. That is absolutely true in the strictest sense, because nobody really knows the future. But it is very important to analyze past performance because it is all we do know with any certainty, and it is generally a reasonably good indicator of the future when all other factors are normal. In general, the longer the history of performance we have, the more accurately it can be used to extrapolate the probable future performance. Virtually any investment will have some history of past performance. If we analyze the actual performance of any investment over a span of several years, we will find its equivalent compound annual growth rate. This is an indication of what the equivalent *fixed* rate of return would have to be to match the *actual* return on that particular investment over a given period of time. For example, if we had invested in the shares of a company like Apple, we could say that the CAGR over the last 20-year timeframe looked like this, as of mid-2024:

12 months	CAGR = 11.27%	$10,000 becomes $11,127 over the past 12 months
3 Years	CAGR = 15.91%	$10,000 becomes $15,572 over the past 3 years
5 Years	CAGR = 35.40%	$10,000 becomes $45,508 over the past 5 years
10 Years	CAGR = 24.14%	$10,000 becomes $86,919 over the past 10 years
15 Years	CAGR = 27.69%	$10,000 becomes $391,159 over the past 15 years
20 Years	CAGR = 35.35%	$10,000 becomes $4,257,603 over the past 20 years

APPL Historical Performance

(AAPL History: *Financecharts.com*, FinanceCharts, 2023, www.fin ancecharts.com/stocks/AAPL/summary/price-cagr. Accessed 6 June 2024.)

These are real historical amounts based on the gains in share value of the company. What this means is that if you owned **APPL** shares for the past year (June 2023 to June 2024), they would be worth 11.27% more at the end of the period; so $10,000 would have turned into $11,127 in one year. If you had owned shares for the past 20 years, they would be worth 35.35% more, on average, *every* year than they did the previous year. That was an absolutely astronomical growth rate. If you had actually invested just $10,000 in Apple 20 years ago it would be worth over $4.25 million today. That's the power of the snowball effect in action, and it is why Apple is currently one of the most valuable companies in the world.

There is even a bonus to this investment that hasn't been mentioned yet. When you are a shareholder, you are literally one of the owners of the company. That means you may be entitled to some of the profits made by the company. Most companies want to grow their revenues as much as possible, so they tend to re-invest their earnings back into their own business. That's a good strategy while they are in a rapid growth phase of their development. It's exactly what Apple did in the early days when they were first developing computers, then iPods, iPads, iPhones, Apple Watches, Apple TV, etc. Now that they make numerous popular consumer electronics devices, and have a huge market share worldwide, they can continue to release new versions of the same products to replace previous versions, and those products will sell like crazy. Apple's growth rate will be very difficult to sustain, but profits should be relatively easy to maintain. In 2012 Apple began paying dividends. This means that every shareholder (part owner) of **APPL** got paid some of the profits each quarter, or more precisely, every time a dividend was declared by the management team, typically on a quarterly basis. The company doesn't pass along all its earnings, because it still does a lot of research and development to stimulate growth, but in most quarters it generates a lot of excess cash and pays some of it to shareholders in the form of dividends. If you had actually purchased $10,000 worth of Apple stock in 2004, not only would those shares be worth almost $4.25 million today, but you would also have been paid some of the earnings every year since 2012. Dividends only add to the snowball effect, especially if you reinvest them to buy even more shares.

An amazing example of the value of dividends is again related to Warren Buffett. He began buying large quantities of shares in Coca-Cola (**KO**) back in 1988 through his holding company, Berkshire Hathaway. Since the early 2000s, Berkshire Hathaway has been receiving more in dividends from Coca-Cola *every year* than the total amount paid for all the **KO** shares. This is in addition to the gain in stock value of about 600% since then.

Any great investment must have the ability to compound its value for shareholders year after year, on average. For the ultimate in gains, the process of reinvesting dividends to buy more shares is like snowball-rolling on steroids. The full snowball effect is therefore the accumulation of gains in share value, plus the dividend payments, plus the dividends reinvested to purchase even more gains in both shares and dividends.

Diversification and a Balanced Portfolio

There is a default principle of traditional investing that we are always reminded of by financial analysts, forecasters, and wealth managers, every time one of their predictions doesn't work out as well as they anticipated; it's the principle of maintaining a balanced portfolio. When they bring this up it is typically combined with the disclaimer that nobody can be right every time. What they really mean is that we should listen to their advice but not follow it with our whole investment portfolio. When they are wrong about a stock recommendation, they want to make it clear that it is still *our* fault, not theirs, if our investment portfolio lost money. A balanced portfolio spreads investments across various asset classes and different types of securities. The idea is that when one stock pick, or even a whole category of securities, does poorly there is likely another investment we could have made that would have performed very well (they often leave it up to us to figure out what those other investments should have been, but with 20/20 hindsight they will point out that an investment in *something-or-other* could have made up for the losses from their recommendation).

The most common recommendations for balanced portfolios are those that contain a mix of stocks and bonds (or the mutual fund equivalents: equity funds and fixed-income funds, which will be explained shortly). It is common knowledge among investment professionals that bonds almost always do well whenever stocks are performing poorly, and vice versa. The reason is easy to understand. When stocks in general significantly drop in value, investors get spooked and want to cut their losses (also known as *stop the bleeding*). This causes a rush to sell their stocks, which drives down prices even further. Once these anxious investors have stopped losing money (by selling their shares) they look for investments that are safe and stable, and will at least make them *some* gains, even if they may not be spectacular. Bonds are just such an investment. Even though bonds are loans that pay fixed interest rates, bond certificates can still be traded on public markets. The interest they pay provides some gains, while the payback of the full value of the loan is guaranteed when the bond matures (as long as the bond issuer, the borrower, hasn't gone bankrupt in the meantime). Therefore, in a bear market (when the general sentiment about the economy is negative, and investors think the value of stocks will be lower in the future) there is always a tidal shift from stocks into bonds. In this situation, the laws of supply and demand will naturally cause stock prices to drop and bond prices to rise. In a bull market, when sentiment (future expectation) turns positive, the tide reverses, causing bond prices to drop while stock prices rise. If this all seems a bit confusing, don't worry; even some professional money managers struggle to understand fixed-income securities.

A very common recommendation made by financial planners is that you should invest about 60% of your portfolio in stocks, or stock mutual funds, and 40% in bonds, or bond mutual funds. They will also say that these percentages should shift for different ages and stages of life. When you are young you can withstand more risk because you have more time to make up for any losses. When you are retired, you are supposed to have already accumulated wealth, so your objective is to keep that wealth and live off the interest it can earn. They therefore advise young investors to put over half of their money into growth stocks, or aggressive growth funds, that are likely to be worth a lot more in the future, but these typically come with the risk of high volatility. They advise retirees to have their portfolios almost entirely in dividend-paying or fixed-income securities, such as bond funds, where losses are far less likely, and the interest being earned can be spent for living expenses instead of reinvested.

That all sounds pretty good in theory but a lot of the incentive behind giving this advice is to protect themselves from any negative consequences of their recommendations. Clients tend to have severe reactions, like moving to a different advisor, or even suing their advisor, if much of their money is lost. As long as there is some growth in portfolio value, advisors are generally safe, so they opt for protecting against losses rather than producing great gains – and they "advise" you to do the same.

If you think about the idea of balancing a portfolio, however, it is almost certain to produce paltry gains. A balanced portfolio can be thought of as a seesaw or teeter-totter. Whenever one child is descending, the kid on the other end is rising. It means that losses in one class of securities will be offset by gains in a sector that performs inversely. In the same way, gains on one side will be tempered by losses in segments that perform inversely. The net results will always be muted. In other words, every time you could have made great gains you won't because there will be losses on the other side of your balanced portfolio. It does keep portfolio volatility lower, but it is not a great recipe for getting rich. Just as every loss you make is offset by gains elsewhere, so every gain you make is diminished by losses elsewhere in your portfolio. A balanced portfolio is a sure recipe for mediocrity, which is not what we want in a long-term investment strategy.

It is important to distinguish between a balanced portfolio and a diversified portfolio. These terms are sometimes used interchangeably but there are crucial differences. Unlike a balanced portfolio, a diversified portfolio doesn't require offsetting one market segment with something that performs inversely. Instead, it just means you don't put all your eggs in one basket. A diversified portfolio can be made up entirely of equities, as long as it is spread across a lot of different stocks. There is no need to include fixed-income securities like bonds or bond mutual funds. In other words, a diversified portfolio is one that contains shares of a great number of different companies in many different kinds of businesses. The benefit is that if one company's shares tumble due to a business flop, it won't have much if any effect on all the other stocks in your portfolio. Of course, there will be economic times during which virtually all stocks will perform poorly. These can be times of bear markets, where the general sentiment of investors is negative, or they can be more severe times of economic recession or depression across the whole country and even the world. The good news is that the *Newborn Nest Egg* formula will allow you to take advantage of these situations wisely, in fact it will be automatic, and should make you delighted.

Dollar Cost Averaging and Buy Low, Sell High

Let's say there was a really nice phone you wanted to buy. Would you get a better deal buying it on the day it is released, or about a year later when it's on a black Friday sale? It is the exact same phone, but you will probably pay around half the price when it's not the absolute latest model, and at a time when stores are anxiously competing for business during the holiday shopping season. Believe it or not, securities can be purchased when they are on sale as well. When it comes to financial success, buying on sale is a great way of cost-saving, and a dollar saved is two dollars earned, even when it comes to saving on investments.

The cardinal rule of investing has always been, "buy low, sell high". It sounds so obvious that very few people even stop to think about what it really means in terms of their investment actions. It is clear that if you buy a stock today, and its price goes up over time, you can sell it later for a higher price than what you paid. Isn't that all there is to it? No, it is not. Heck, even gambling could be successful if you were always able to quit while you were ahead. There are specific strategies for using the buy low, sell high principle to your advantage. Rigorous analysis is the appropriate strategy for short-term investment decisions, while dollar cost averaging automates the principle for long-term investments.

For short-term decisions, some investors, or investment prognosticators, put a lot of energy into predicting which direction individual stocks are about to move, where we are in a given financial cycle, or where the greatest dangers and opportunities lie. Making these predictions usually focuses on one of two strategies: analyzing "fundamentals" or performing "technical analysis". Both of these require a lot of time and effort, and are therefore expensive.

Fundamental analysis focuses on the financial health of the company, its price-to-earnings (P/E) ratio, and its growth potential due to specific product developments, marketing strategies, mergers, acquisitions, divestitures, or other business strategies. It attempts to analyze whether the stock is currently overpriced or underpriced relative to the intrinsic value of the company, and therefore predict whether it is more likely to go down versus up. The sentiment of investors is not really factored into the analysis of fundamentals because it is believed by these analysts that sentiment is more or less unpredictable.

Technical analysis, on the other hand, focuses on movements in the price of a stock, and even of entire stock indices. It uses recent stock or index price movements to gauge momentum trends, support levels, resistance levels, breakout levels, and other price-pattern indicators. Technical analysis doesn't look at any financial or business fundamentals that might indicate the particulars of how well the company is performing; it doesn't even care what industry a company is in. Instead, it focuses almost entirely on patterns of price momentum, so this accounts for investor sentiment more than any other factor. It tries to identify the upcoming results of herd mentality.

All of this effort, and its associated cost, can be avoided by investors with long-term outlooks because it can be automated. A powerful strategy that adds a great deal to the snowball effect is called *dollar cost averaging*. This is an important component of the Newborn Nest Egg formula because it gives you a huge benefit when stock markets go *down*! The longer your investment runway, the better this strategy will work because there is more time to exercise it. It is based on two factors: 1) regular contributions of the same dollar amounts to your investment fund, and 2) buying things when they are on sale instead of paying full price.

The primary reason behind this opportunity is that stock and bond prices are based at least as much on the sentiment of investors as on the companies' financial health, intrinsic value, or even the economy of the country. Investor sentiment is swayed by all kinds of things that may not affect the profitability or growth of the company at all. Sentiment is tied to things like general economic conditions in the country or the world, pandemics, wars, stock market momentum, shifts from stocks into bonds, and vice versa, legal issues or potential lawsuits against companies, accounting anomalies, news, fake news, postings on Reddit, and market segment popularity caused by breakthroughs in medicine, technology, or cryptocurrency. The net effect of all these sentiment-driven moves is that stock prices can be "on-sale" compared to the intrinsic value of the companies.

Another factor is that stock prices tend to move in tandem, creating a cyclical effect. Sentiment seldom affects just one stock. It often affects the whole stock market, or at least a whole market segment. For example, if Silicon Valley Bank collapses (as it did in 2023), investors tend to dive out of all bank stocks as a knee-jerk reaction. The sentiment is that other banks may not really be in good shape financially, other banks are about to fail (and we don't know which ones), or primarily that a bunch of other investors will be exiting their positions in bank stocks so all bank share prices will inevitably fall. This is called *running for the exits; w*hoever pulls the sell trigger first gets to keep more of their money.

Sentiment can cause shares to go on sale, but it can have the opposite effect as well. When too many investors have an enthusiastic outlook about a particular stock, or the overall market, it can be priced at a premium. It would be like buying a pair of tickets to a Taylor Swift concert way in advance, at the list price, then selling them later to some desperate mom who wants to impress her Swiftie daughter but hasn't planned ahead. She needs two tickets urgently and will pay anything. You can therefore sell her the tickets you bought low, and demand a high premium: same tickets, different value, all because of a change in sentiment.

Great investors also believe they must be contrarians – doing the opposite of what everybody else is doing. They try to buy low, when nobody else wants to buy, and sell high when everybody else wants to buy. Our favorite poster boy of investing, Warren Buffett, famously says, "Be fearful when others are greedy and greedy when others are fearful." Great advice if you have billions of dollars in reserves like he does, and you can pounce on opportunities that nobody else can afford. For instance, he plowed $3 billion into General Electric at the height of the 2008 financial crisis. He received $3 billion worth of preferred stock paying a 10% annual dividend, plus stock warrants that allowed him to buy more shares at his initial purchase price even if the future stock price was higher. Ultimately Buffett's company, Berkshire Hathaway, made about $1.5 billion in profit on this deal, that's a 50% ROI in short order! The challenge for us retail investors is that we can't all be contrarian. If we were, we'd simply be following the crowd, also known as herd mentality, which is the opposite of being contrarian.

All of this background is provided so that the concept of dollar cost averaging can be well understood. Intuitively we can see that volatility and investor sentiment are very difficult to predict. The reason is that there are just too many variables; too many factors that can change overnight. If you were to look at historical stock market data, and could compare it to predictions, it would be clear that, as Yogi Berra once said, "It's tough to make predictions, especially about the future". The good news is that with enough time on your side, it isn't necessary to *make* such predictions in order to *take advantage* of them.

The process of dollar cost averaging is extremely simple, yet very powerful for investors with a long enough runway. It involves just picking an enduring investment and making a commitment to add an equal amount of money to that investment every month for a very long time.

Picking such an investment is not as hard as it sounds. You simply ask yourself one simple question: will this entity still be surviving and thriving in 50 to 100 years? This is exactly what Warren (we're imagining we're on a first-name basis now) asked himself about Coca-Cola before he invested billions in **KO** and became its largest shareholder. Of course you have to be very sure you are right about the answer to that 50 to 100 year question. For us, who don't have billions to invest in a contrarian move over a short period of time like Warren does, we can use the dollar cost averaging process to accumulate our holdings; a steady monthly addition to the same investment.

Here is how it works, and why it works so well for the young investor, especially one as young as your child. For an enduring investment that is sure to last and prosper over decades, there will be cycles of overly positive sentiment, when the investment is overpriced, and periods of very negative sentiment when it goes on sale. If you invest the same dollar amount every month over the long term, you don't care whether the price is up or down in the short term, even if the investment seems to be irrationally priced for long stretches of time. If you are buying when the price is high, you can celebrate the fact that all your previous purchases of this investment have made great gains. If you are buying when the price is ludicrously low, you know you are buying at fire-sale prices, and are loading up for massive future gains.

Even if a decade or more of investing with dollar cost averaging produces losses or paltry gains, this is the <u>ideal scenario</u> because it means you have been buying at sale prices the whole time. You have accumulated a lot more shares per dollar in this situation than you would have if share prices had been steadily rising during this time.

Dollar cost averaging allows you to take advantage of the first half of the contrarian investor's creed as you accumulate your holdings, you are often *buying low*. And you accomplish this with great efficiency without trying to predict the future. Believe me, you will be buying low much more efficiently than the best stock analysts, even those who claim to specialize in contrarian advice. These analysts have to try to predict future sentiment, which is unreliable, and then try to be contrarian, much like everybody else. With the accumulation strategy of dollar cost averaging, you will automatically take advantage of the opportunity to buy on sale every time there is a financial crisis, pandemic, war, recession, or a sideways market that has no distinct bull or bear direction.

The most profound benefit of dollar cost averaging is that it frees you from fretting about what the market is doing. You don't have to listen to stock market updates, subscribe to economic newsletters, study the performance of key companies, or even keep track of the major market indexes. All kinds of things affect these numbers, but they don't matter to you in terms of influencing your actions. It is wise to have some understanding of what drives stock prices so that you won't be spooked when someone says, "this time it's different". The fact is that economic times have changed in every generation, usually several times per generation, and they always will. Ultimately stock prices move based on supply and demand, just like the price of everything else in a free market economy (government interference aside – but that's a topic for a different book). The performance of individual companies, world events, and the sentiment of investors all sway the demand side of that equation, sometimes in extreme and irrational ways, but eventually prices correct based on the intrinsic value of the key industries in the world economy. Dollar cost averaging lets you confidently ride-out irrational pricing with conviction in your long-term strategy.

But how do you accomplish the second half of the strategy; selling high? Ahhh, you are asking very wise questions now, but the answer might be quite unexpected:

The best way to sell high is to never sell! Why would you ever fire your most productive employees?

Once you have a magnificent-sized snowball rolling along, passively compounding your wealth, there is no necessity to keep contributing a few dollars per month to boost your investment; at that point it boosts itself. As I've said before, your first $million is the hardest to make. For example, you don't really need to keep adding to your own nest egg once your snowball is growing at a healthy rate, with average gains that vastly outpace your monthly contribution. Once you've reached that level of wealth you can start to pull some of your investment profits off the table. You can spend more for other things of value to your lifestyle, like travel, fine dining, luxury items, charities, or even living expenses, but leave the vast majority of your money working for you. This will provide you with a generous income, protection from inflation, and generational wealth you can leave to your kids and grandkids. As our implicit friend and mentor, Warren, is fond of saying, "My favorite holding period is *forever.*"

Don't Lose Money

This topic doesn't sound like anything worth discussing because it's so obvious, but again, for most people there will be some aspects of this section that will reveal insights they have never realized before.

This topic is critical to understand so that it provides the necessary deterrent to getting involved in risky investments, especially with a significant

**portion of your portfolio, which could lead to
devastating consequences.**

Because we are human, we can't seem to extricate our emotions from
our actions, no matter how firmly we believe we can. This could lead
us to extremely unfavorable results whenever our investment decisions
seem to turn against us. When we make any decision, we like to think
it's the right one, which can lead us to "throw good money after bad"
just to prove that our initial judgment was right.

I worked in Silicon Valley, riding the tech industry wave during the
dot.com boom of the late 1990s through to its bust in the early 2000s.
As with most executives in that era, I was given stock options as a
signing bonus. At more than one point my options were worth $millions, but there were restrictions on exercising them because of the
regulations against insider trading. (Exercising options means buying the allotted shares at the option price and simultaneously selling
them at current market value.) I was eventually able to exercise some
options and make significant gains. But shortly thereafter I became
so convinced that the dot.com companies were doomed that I began
selling short. This is a strategy that makes gains only if the share
price goes down. I was betting against the very industry I worked in.
Unfortunately, I started too late, and many share prices had already
bottomed out. I ended up losing most of the gains I had made, which
were nowhere near what my options had been worth at the peak of
the dot.com market frenzy. I thought that since I had missed the top,
I would try to make maximum gains as share prices dropped. I missed
the timing again and lost almost as much as I had managed to gain with
my stock options. If only I had been dollar cost averaging in long-term
investments instead, I would have been buying tremendous quantities

of great shares while they were on sale. Imagine the gains of **APPL** and **MSFT** since then!

If you study the actions people take, and the lengths to which they will go to justify their decisions, it can become quite comical – unless it's you. A phrase I have come up with to describe this behavior is: *most people would rather be right than rich*. The CEO of a company I worked for was once evaluating a very substantial offer from a potential customer to purchase a multimillion-dollar contract of goods and services we provided. I knew our costs to fulfill the contract, and the price other customers had typically paid for similar projects, so I knew the offer we had in hand could be a lucrative deal for us. Our CEO wouldn't budge from the amount quoted in our bid, however, because he was trying to make a point to the prospective customer. The reason? The prospective customer was a business rival of his. Our CEO and his rival saw themselves in a negotiation contest with each other. Unfortunately, the rival did not become a customer because he had other supplier options. He undoubtedly paid more to the alternative contractor, and received inferior products and services, but in his mind, he had proven to himself that he was the better negotiator - as had our CEO apparently. Both rivals would rather be right than rich. Try your best to overcome the emotions that compel humans to make these kinds of financial blunders. The good news is that a set-and-forget strategy like the *Newborn Nest Egg* formula effectively removes emotions from *all* your investment decisions.

Let's explore the principle further with a few investment hypotheticals. Let's say that you made an investment of $10,000 and it lost $2,000 of its value; a loss of 20%. The question is, what percentage would you have to gain on your remaining $8,000 investment to break even? The answer is you would have to gain 25%. That doesn't seem fair, does it? But the math is easy. Your investment value is now down to $8,000, and the $2,000 gain required to break even is 1/4, or 25%, of $8,000. So it's true – if you lose 20% you will have to make 25% just to break even, but it gets much worse. If you were to lose 1/3 of your $10,000, which is $3,333. You now have 2/3 of your money left. How much do you need to gain to break even? Well, you have two times as much left as what you lost, and you will have to gain one-half of that back in order to break even, so that's a 50% gain. Yup, losing 33.3% requires a 50% ROI just to break even. But the deeper we go the worse it gets; losing 50% requires a 100% gain to break even. That's not something that is likely to happen so a lot of investors in this situation "stop the bleeding" and sell the remainder of their position. Then they move what funds they have left into something that actually has the possibility of doubling their money because emotionally they just have to make up for their loss. These kinds of returns are alleged to be possible in more volatile (meaning risky) investments. But volatile investments are just as likely to lose another 50% before they make any gains. It literally becomes desperation investing at that point, and it typically ends the same as a gambling addiction; the house always wins. Desperate people do desperate things!

Just to pound this point home with one last example, let's say you lost 90% of your investment. Now what does it take to break even? In some investments, losses like this aren't as unrealistic as they might sound. There are even cases of iconic companies that are famous for it:

- **Washington Mutual (2008):** Washington Mutual, a large U.S. savings and loan bank, faced severe problems during the financial crisis and was seized by regulators in September 2008. Its stock price, which had been over $30 per share in 2007, became virtually worthless.

- **General Motors (2008-2009):** General Motors, one of the largest automakers in the world, faced financial distress during the 2008-2009 financial crisis. The stock dropped from over $40 per share in 2007 to less than $2 per share in 2009. GM eventually filed for bankruptcy in 2009.

- **Valeant Pharmaceuticals (2015-2016):** Valeant faced controversy over its business practices and accounting issues. The stock, which had reached over $250 per share in 2015, fell dramatically to less than $10 in 2016.

It's not impossible to recover from a 90% loss but the chances are extremely slim. If a stock dropped by 90% and you hung on to it because the company still survived, it would have to make gains of 1,000% just to break even. How realistic is that?

It is exactly these dangers that will cause wise *Newborn Nest Egg* investors to use two of the strategies mentioned previously, diversification and dollar cost averaging, to ensure they don't lose money. These strategies virtually guarantee you will never dig a hole so deep that you resort to desperate measures to recover. This one-two punch will ensure that no single company with weak performance or some kind of fraudulent behavior will sink your portfolio. The greatest danger stock-pickers have, or those who follow their advice, is a relatively small portfolio containing just a handful of stocks. If just one goes against the selection thesis, it can be devastating. A very broadly diversified portfolio is a fantastic way to avoid the pitfalls of desperation investing. And when widespread economic circumstances knock your whole portfolio down, negative sentiment will allow you to buy shares while they are on sale. Following the principles of buy-low-sell-high through dollar cost averaging, you will make fantastic gains once the negative sentiment turns around.

Know When to Hold 'Em

How are you, as a retail investor, to distinguish between the wisdom of dollar cost averaging, which allows you to buy shares when they are on sale, and the concept of not losing money, which often leads to desperation investing? The answer is as simple as this: If you are invested in an individual company, dollar cost averaging is a bad strategy in almost every case, whereas if your investment is very widely diversified, dollar cost averaging across your whole portfolio provides the benefits of buying shares at attractive prices. What makes all the difference is whether you ever have to sell the investment. One way to look at this is that if you never sell you can never really lose money. Losing money is based on the difference between your entry price point and a lower exit price.

Does this mean you should never sell a losing investment? Absolutely not; sometimes it is necessary to stop the bleeding. That can be much better than throwing good money after bad. But this situation only really comes up with investments in individual securities or a small handful of stocks. That's why a widely diversified portfolio is the only recommendation for the set-and-forget *Newborn Nest Egg* formula. If the whole economy, and therefore the broad market (i.e., the S&P 500) drops in price, buy it when it's on sale. The broad market very closely tracks the economy as a whole. Unless America itself disintegrates, the broad market will reflect the economy, and the economy will inevitably recover. If it doesn't, we have bigger problems than money can solve.

The important thing to understand is that investing in individual securities takes a lot of time, effort, research, knowledge, experience, guidance, and luck. That kind of direction comes from different books than this one, and they don't remain relevant for very long because times change. For our purposes, we will always work with very widely diversified investments, and won't be recommending entry and exit points in terms of prices or timing. We will use a buy-and-hold strategy for which dollar cost averaging is the ideal accumulation method.

What this means, however, is that a long time-horizon is the only one for which the *Newborn Nest Egg* formula works reliably. I do not recommend it for runways shorter than about 25 years. It also means that there can be long periods of time when it feels like the process isn't working. These are the times when your resolve needs to be absolute. Continue to buy regularly and resolutely through the lengthy times of low or negative growth using the dollar cost averaging strategy. These will ultimately turn out to be your best buying opportunities.

Think about the numerous challenges to the US economy, and therefore to investing in the broad market, since the year 2000. First was the dot.com bust, then the Enron scandal, next was 9-11, then we experienced the gut-wrenching 2008 global financial crisis, after that was COVID-19, followed immediately by a war in Ukraine, leading to global supply chain disasters, leading to a spike in inflation, followed by a war in Gaza, and the threat of wars in Taiwan, North Korea, Iran, etc., etc. Incidents and situations like these are unlikely to ever go out of style. If those disruptive events had discouraged investment, the greatest buying opportunities of our generation would have been squandered. But continuing to buy steadily through all that turmoil is not for the faint of heart.

Take a look at the chart below showing the S&P 500 from January 2000 to June 2024.

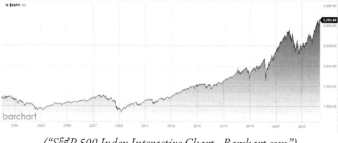

("S&P 500 Index Interactive Chart - Barchart.com")

If an investor had started buying in the year 2000, there would have been no gains at all, and some terrifying downturns, from then until 2013, yet the 24-year CAGR of this broad market has still been better than 10% since 2000. Notice specifically the massive dip from 2008 to 2009. The S&P 500 lost 50% of its value during the global financial crisis. What a magnificent buying opportunity that was! When extended periods of buying stocks on sale are experienced, it indicates a buildup of pent-up demand that will power the market higher when sentiment reverses. With the very long runway of the *Newborn Nest Egg* strategy, time is on our side.

Look at it from another perspective. Let's say you happened to start investing in the S&P 500 at the depth of the aftermath of the global financial crisis – 2009 (by buying shares of an ETF that provides investment in all 500 companies in the market index simultaneously). The CAGR since that time has been over 15%, so the return on your 2009 investment would have been over 800% so far. By the rule of 72, your money would have doubled every 4.8 years, on average, since

2009. Even if you started investing before that, and stuck diligently to your dollar cost averaging strategy, some of your investments would indeed have been made when stocks were being offered at their deepest discount prices. That is how fantastic gains are made; without any research, analysis, financial advice, or studying economists' reports. It also eliminates the fees, time consumption, and anxiety that can accompany other investment strategies. If you have no deadline or pressure to sell or exit your positions, time is on your side. Sometimes it takes balls of steel (no sexism intended), but the combination of a very long runway and the power of dollar cost averaging in widely diversified investments has always proven to produce remarkable gains.

Countdown to Launch

If you have already determined to set aside some money for your children's education, graduation, and wedding, you are way ahead of most new parents. That's a great start but it's what you do with those allocated funds that will make all the difference. Even if you haven't yet managed to set aside some specific funds, you can still be magnanimous parents who launch their kids into adulthood with a solid financial foundation and the skills to grow that base of wealth into financial independence and beyond. To achieve both objectives it is important to put the *Newborn Nest Egg* formula into effect now, as far in advance as possible, then teach it to your kids before handing over their million-dollar or multimillion-dollar nest egg. Just to be clear, the *Newborn Nest Egg* formula is not meant to replace the funds needed for your kids' education and other life milestones; it is meant to be additional, but the same investment techniques could be used for both if you start when they are newborns. And as you will soon see, you can afford to do both.

The upcoming chapter will present the steps you can implement immediately, with the objective of creating a structure that can be passed on to your kids at the time of your choosing. The principles will be targeted at you, so that you can learn them, apply them, practice them, and refine them for your particular situation. As soon as you do that, your family will have a safety nest in place because your money will be working tirelessly at growing the nest egg. The beauty of the system is that for whatever level of wealth you choose to target, you can set it and forget it. You may set up a simple one-million-dollar wealth target for yourselves and each of your children, or you might aim for multiples of that. Either way, at some point your kids will need to understand what you have unleashed for them so they can carry it on, and preferably add to it. They can then pass on family wealth and financial management wisdom for generations to come.

CHAPTER 16

STACKS OF GREEN

Thomas Edison experimented with many different materials before he found a suitable filament for his electric light bulb. It is commonly cited that he spent years, and large sums of money, testing over 6,000 different materials, including cedar, cotton, and bamboo, as well as metals like platinum and iridium. Eventually, he settled on carbonized bamboo as the filament material, which proved to be durable and efficient enough for use in his commercially viable electric light bulb. Incandescent bulbs based on his original design are still produced today, although filaments are now typically made of tungsten. A conservative estimate would be that fifty billion dollars worth of incandescent bulbs have been sold in the US alone.

Imagine if someone from the future could have revealed to Edison exactly what material to use as a filament before he spent all that time and money on research. What a windfall that would have been; something so simple providing such monumental value. The wealth-building formula that is about to be described is similarly simple and valuable.

From what you have read so far, you're probably thinking there hasn't been any earth-shattering secret revealed that will instantly enable you to create million-dollar nest eggs for your kids. In fact, it may sound suspiciously boring compared to the stories you hear about crypto wealth, day trading, Reddit-fueled social momentum strategies, or viral social media sensations. Well, that's true because with investing, boring can be great while earth-shattering can be devastating. With the background you have learned so far, and the steps you are about to take to put them into practice, the *Newborn Nest Egg* formula is virtually guaranteed to generate million-dollar nest eggs, and most likely multimillion. Even if you create only million-dollar nest eggs yourself, you can still gift those to your kids and teach them to manage this foundational wealth and grow it into multimillion-dollar territory. As mentioned previously, a great way to give the knowledge portion of your nest egg gift is by getting your kids to read this book, or by providing them with the next book in the *FAST Wealth* series when they are about sixteen. You can find that book at www.FastWealth.com.

The steps that will be outlined here can be used to simultaneously generate wealth for yourselves and for your kids. Some parents assume that they should just generate wealth for themselves throughout their lives, then bequeath it all to their kids in their will. That's fair enough but it's missing at least two key components. Having a safety nest set aside specifically for each child throughout their lives, teaching them to manage it, and letting them experience the discipline and rewards of continuing its growth, is worth much more than just a bag of money when you die. Secondly, if you live a full, long life, your kids may never get to retire early and start doing what they love before they are elderly themselves. A true safety nest is worth much more to them, and to you as well, because it maintains the lifelong family bond of working cooperatively on building a financial foundation.

What a great pursuit to have in common with your kids throughout their adult lives; not just the accumulation of wealth but the wisdom of how to use it for good, and how to pass it on to future generations. Generating nest eggs for your children doesn't necessarily have to be in separate accounts in their names, although that could keep things clear in terms of ownership. It may be worth getting professional tax advice to figure out the best account structures for your own nest egg and those for your kids. Don't put off initiating the process though; tax advice can always come later. If you just start with all accounts in your own names, as parents, you maintain control of when to turn over responsibility to each of your kids. When you decide to transfer ownership of an account, in accounting terms it will be considered a gift between family members, which can be structured as a non-taxable event.

An important bit of wealth wisdom to learn for yourself first, and then instill in your children, is the key to honest wealth. It is important to respect and appreciate wealth so that when you achieve it you hang on to it and multiply it. How many stories have you heard about lottery winners who suddenly have a million or a few million dollars but then go broke within a year? The underlying reason is that they don't realize how rare it is to have wealth. They didn't earn it by following a strategy and committing to it unconditionally. They got it so easily that they think it will readily happen again if they ever run out of money. They feel entitled to money, like for them it was just "meant to be" and believe they have so much that it will never run out – and they spend accordingly. They have never learned basic financial management principles or what honest wealth really means. How sad would it be if you invested on behalf of your kids for 16 years or more and all they did when they received the gift was blow it all on cars, gadgets, and partying.

I knew of a family who lived in a trailer park and inherited something like $100,000 when a relative died. This seemed like a fortune to them, and they just *knew* that the deceased would have wanted them to have something really nice. So the husband immediately went out and bought his dream car, a 20-year-old Corvette. The wife then found the car of her dreams, a Mustang GT of the same era. In their world, these were status symbols. In reality, their expenses had just begun because muscle cars of that vintage cost a lot for gas, insurance, maintenance, and repairs. The family's new-found money was soon gone, and their status symbols probably didn't impress their neighbors nearly as much as they hoped. All they had to show for their inheritance was depreciating assets and increased expenses.

True wealth is a mindset, and this is important to put into practice yourself, and then teach your kids: If every month your net worth is the highest it has ever been, then every month you are the richest you have ever been. This is honest wealth. It is what makes you feel wealthy, and it provides all the other beneficial symptoms of honest wealth: confidence, self-assurance, admiration and respect from others, the ability to be generous, and above all, low stress levels. In this situation, when you have structured your life and managed your finances yourself to create honest wealth, nothing in your day-to-day work life or job situation can bother you much or make you anxious or stressed. That, in itself, has great value. It is a very likable quality as long as you don't get cocky or arrogant about it. You will find it easy to get along with others who understand the same principles as you do, and are financially self-sufficient like you are.

Our favorite wealth icon, Warren Buffett, one of the world's richest people, still lives in the same, relatively modest house he bought in 1958 for $31,500, drives ordinary cars like Chevys or Toyotas, wears off-the-shelf suits instead of tailor-made, often flies commercial instead of on private jets, and is fond of cheeseburgers, milkshakes, and Cherry Coke. Of course his company, Berkshire Hathaway, is a major shareholder of both Coca-Cola and Dairy Queen, but you get the point.

OK, enough with the psychology lessons, let's continue with the financial lessons and show you how to lay a nice golden nest egg. The following step-by-step guide must be understood as an example only, not as specific financial advice. The reason is that only those who are licensed to provide financial advice are allowed by law to do so, and that's not me. It is all those financial planners and wealth management professionals who get paid by financial product providers to sell you whatever makes them the most money or perks. They can legally give you financial advice, even though it is typically of more benefit to themselves than to you. I can't do that, but I *can* tell you about my own experiences, and that's where the following example comes from.

These steps will bypass the whole financial planning, advisory, and wealth management industry that was explained earlier. It also eliminates all their associated costs, and puts control of your wealth into your own hands. This follows one of the first principles laid out in this book; your financial success is completely your own responsibility, nobody else's. It is also much more cost-effective because the whole cost of mutual funds, asset management companies, and other financial infrastructure is eliminated. It also follows every one of the wealth-building and preserving principles taught so far. So here is the investment portion of the *Newborn Nest Egg* formula in a nutshell. It is a step-by-step *example* of how you can ensure with virtual certainty that you will generate your own, and your children's, million-dollar nest eggs, and you can do it *today*!

The Ten-Step Formula

1. **Generate Income.** Unless someone gives you money or you win a lottery (which you won't because you are wise enough to know that lotteries, like gambling, are just expensive hobbies) your jobs will be the source of steady household income for now. If you can't earn something like the average full-time worker, your first priority might be to develop the skills necessary to secure such a job. On the other hand, you are about to be shocked at how little you need to invest to lock-in a million-dollar safety nest for your family. If your jobs don't pay an average American income (or the equivalent in your country) and it's unrealistic to find higher-paying jobs, don't despair. Over the next few pages you will see the amount you will need to invest per month, based on the current age of your kids, to secure a million dollars for your family by retirement age or earlier. You can even secure multimillion-dollar nest eggs with your current jobs if you diligently work through your budget and find ways to cut costs, and/or add income until your bottom line allows you to make the required investment commitment. Don't take no for an answer. This is where you gotta *want* it!

2. **Make a Household Budget.** You can always use the sample budget presented earlier in this book as a template, but make it specific to your circumstances. You can download a copy of

the sample spreadsheet from www.NewbornNestEgg.com. Enter your own line items for both income and expenses, then adjust your expenses, both fixed and discretionary, as necessary to ensure that you live honestly within your means while boosting your bottom line as much as possible. All of financial management is making tradeoffs of one expense versus another. If you can produce a workable remainder, don't worry too much about generating extra income for now. Remember that cost-saving is twice as valuable as a pay raise in terms of increasing your bottom line. Reduce as many of your expenses as you can to ensure the remainder at the bottom line of your budget is as large as possible. If you can't seem to get a positive remainder, read the next book in the *FAST Wealth* series. It contains several ideas for both cost-savings and income generation. Details can be found at www.FastWealth.com.

3. **Commit to Savings.** Once you have completed your budget, found as many cost-saving opportunities as possible, and adjusted your expenses to ensure a healthy remainder every month, you are already rich. If all you do is commit to saving that remainder, then every month you are the richest you have ever been. Knowing you are always the richest you have ever been, that each month thereafter you will be even richer, and that you took the responsibility to do it yourself, makes you honestly wealthy. The important thing is to make this amount of money your absolute, unwavering commitment to wealth generation for your family's future. The next step is to put that money to work and start growing a snowball that increases your wealth exponentially.

4. **Select a Single S&P 500 ETF** for all your investments (for both spouses and for your kids). It is the ideal investment for the long-term *Newborn Nest Egg* strategy (the reasons will be clarified further in the remainder of this book). This will be your investment of choice for all the accounts listed in the steps below: 401(k)(or the equivalent in your country), IRA (or the equivalent in your country), and cash investments. It is important that your chosen ETF has an option for automatically reinvesting dividends so that you get the maximum growth rate of your snowball. Any of the following ETFs can be found and traded in virtually any brokerage account, which you will set up in step 7:

   a. **SPDR S&P 500 ETF Trust (SPY):** This is one of the most popular S&P 500 ETFs. It tracks the performance of the S&P 500 Index and allows reinvesting dividends.

   b. **iShares Core S&P 500 ETF (IVV):** Another widely used ETF that aims to replicate the performance of the S&P 500. It is known for its low expense ratio.

   c. **Vanguard S&P 500 ETF (VOO):** Vanguard's S&P 500 ETF is known for its low expense ratio and aims to closely track the S&P 500. Dividends can be reinvested.

5. **Take Advantage of Any 401(k)** plans offered by your employers (both spouses), especially if the employers match or make contributions on your behalf. This will defer your income taxes until years later when you withdraw the money, hopefully in your retirement. Both spouses should authorize the maximum allowable payroll deductions for deposit into

these accounts. Get self-directed 401(k) accounts if they are available to you in any way. You may need to meet with your HR manager but do everything you can to get control of where your 401(k) contributions are invested. Have all of both spouses' 401(k) contributions, plus any matching contributions your employers make, invested in your chosen S&P 500 ETF from step 4 above. If self-managed (self-directed) investments such as ETFs are not available to you, select an available mutual fund or managed fund that most closely resembles an S&P 500 ETF. It must be very broadly diversified, contain equities only (no balancing components like bonds or fixed-income funds), have exceedingly low management/maintenance fees, no front-end or back-end loads (described in Appendix A), and reinvest dividends. If your 401(k) investments (both spouses) are your entire monthly commitment for growing your own nest egg, as distinct from those for your kids, that's fine, especially if you have additional pension plans through your employers. The remaining steps of the *Newborn Nest Egg* formula will explain how to make additional automated investments.

a. Note that if you reside in the UK, the nearest equivalent to a 401(k) is called a Self-Invested Personal Pension (SIPP), in Australia it is called Self-Managed Superannuation Funds (SMSFs), and in Canada it is called a Registered Retirement Savings Plan (RRSP).

b. Many other countries have similar government-supported structures designed to encourage investing for retirement by deferring or reducing income taxes. In most cases, the money contributed to these retirement accounts is limited to a percentage of income, and your contributions are either pre-tax (deducted by your employer) or tax-deductible (claimed on your annual Income Tax filing) in the year they are contributed. Taxes are then paid when money is withdrawn, usually in retirement when income from other sources may be lower, so your tax bracket may be lower. Typically, no taxes are paid on the gains made by the investments in these accounts until money is withdrawn, and in some cases, not even then.

6. **Open Individual Retirement Accounts (IRAs)** for each spouse, typically through your bank. Automate the transfer of funds from your main bank account into these IRA accounts every month. Make monthly contributions that add up to the maximum allowable annual contribution for each spouse, if your committed investment amount is sufficient. An IRA is particularly important if you do not have traditional employment where your employer offers a 401(k) plan; it is allowable to have both. A Roth IRA will generally be the best choice because, although contributions will not be tax-deductible, the gains made in these accounts are tax-free upon withdrawal. Once you see (later in this chapter) the gains you will be making, you will understand the great value of being able to withdraw this money tax-free in the future.

   a. Having both 401(k) accounts and Roth IRA accounts might be a convenient way to distinguish between funds in your own nest egg versus those designated for your kids: 401(k)s for yourselves, and Roth IRAs for dividing between your own and your kids' nest eggs. Be cautious about opening child/custodial Roth IRAs because laws strictly limit your contributions and your choice of timing in turning over control of those accounts to your children. It's much more flexible to keep the IRA account in your own name until you determine when you want to turn over control of nest eggs to your kids. Even at that point, you may not want to transfer all funds to them at once because there could be gift-tax implications, and maybe even the temptation for your kids to start spending their money (see step 10 below).

b. Note that in the UK, the nearest equivalent to a Roth IRA is called an Individual Savings Account (ISA), in Canada it is called a Tax Free Savings Account (TFSA), and in Australia the Self-Managed Superannuation Fund (SMSF) has options that allow an individual's contributions to be treated similarly to a Roth IRA.

c. Many other countries have government-supported plans similar to Roth IRAs. Take advantage of contributing to these in every way possible in your country, and make the same S&P 500 ETF investments with the money you deposit into these accounts.

7. **Get an Online Brokerage Account.** Presumably you have a bank account, ideally a joint account with your spouse; that's where all your household income should go every month. Your bank will very likely have an online banking system, and will offer brokerage accounts as part of that system. If so, this brokerage account may be a good choice because it will

provide a convenient, automated way to transfer money between accounts. Bank brokerage accounts sometimes charge fees per trade, and you will typically be doing a few trades per month (depending on how many IRA and cash investment accounts you set up). Brokerage account fees are something to research because some of the apps and web accounts that don't charge for trades have hidden costs such as deposit and withdrawal fees. Just know that commission-free is not necessarily the same as absolutely free. Find a brokerage account that is free, or as inexpensive as possible, because even a few bucks per transaction or per month can significantly reduce your long-term returns, as you're about to see. If your bank doesn't offer a good online brokerage account, or even if it does and you prefer something simple and easy to access from your phone, here are a few other suggestions:

a. **Robinhood:** Known for its commission-free trading, Robinhood is popular among users who prefer a simple and easy-to-use platform. It may lack some of the advanced features provided by other brokerages but is easily adequate for the *Newborn Nest Egg* strategy.

b. **Webull:** Another commission-free platform that caters to both beginners and active traders.

c. **E*TRADE (now part of Morgan Stanley):** Provides a variety of tools and educational resources. E*TRADE has been known for its user-friendly platform and strong mobile app. Just don't get sidetracked by all the available investment services and advice; those are designed to extract additional ongoing fees from your portfolio.

8. **Link Your Brokerage Account to your IRA accounts.** Set your brokerage account to automatically invest each month's IRA contributions into your chosen S&P 500 ETF. If you can't automate the transfers or investments, set a monthly reminder on your phone, Google Calendar, or somewhere to help ensure that you *never* forget your monthly investment commitment. You will be most successful if this step is fully automated, so find a way to make that happen if at all possible. That's the only true set-and-forget approach. It frees you from facing the decision every month of opting to spend the money instead of investing it. Be sure to select the option for reinvesting dividends.

9. **Automate Your Cash Investments.** If your commitment to growing nest eggs for your family allows for greater investment than the maximum allowable 401(k) and Roth IRA contributions (or whatever tax-deferred and tax-free investment plans are available in your country), make the remaining investments from your bank account. Set your brokerage account to automatically invest your additional committed amount from your bank account into your selected S&P 500 ETF every month. Be sure to select the option for reinvesting dividends.

10. **Get Tax Advice** (but not investment advice) from your accountant regarding the most advantageous structure of your family's 401(k)s, Roth IRAs, and possible child/custodial Roth IRAs. Every family's circumstances are different when it comes to the most favorable tax-deferred or tax-free investment accounts. If you operate a family business it is particularly important that you seek professional tax guidance

because in this case contributions to your children's nest eggs may be made in Custodial Roth IRA(s) in your kids' names. The *Newborn Nest Egg* formula will generate tremendous wealth, and your accountant's job is to ensure that you and your kids get to keep as much of it as possible.

  a. If you are a foreign investor (investing in the S&P 500 as a citizen of a country other than the US), it is also critical to get advice from a tax professional. Ensure that your accountant or tax advisor is skilled in US investment rules to ensure you keep the maximum possible amount of your gains.

Anticipated Results

How exactly do these ten steps complete the process of setting up the investment portion of the *Newborn Nest Egg formula*? The principle works like this: If you commit the appropriate amount of funds every month to buying shares of an S&P 500 ETF, and you stick to your plan long-term, you are virtually guaranteed to have your million-dollar, or multimillion-dollar, nest egg set aside for your own as well as your child's retirement. Once you set up this strategy and carry it out, preferably with completely automated processes, you can mentally put it in a box on a shelf and call it a nest egg. It is much like a loan of millions of dollars that you have made to someone, but it won't be paid back till retirement. You can count its full future value as an asset today in net worth calculations even though the money can't be spent until it is paid out. It is similar to owning a multimillion-dollar government long-bond that won't pay out for 30 years or so. It is already a multimillion-dollar asset, it's just not liquid. Once you see how powerfully this nest egg grows you will want to add to it, both for your own retirement and for your children's.

This investment strategy might sound too easy or maybe too boring, but that's exactly the point. You may have seen the numerous blogs, posts, podcasts, and YouTube videos that give similar investment advice, and you assume it can't be that easy so these "gurus" must be missing something. You may have also seen the derogatory opposing views posted by other "experts", claiming it's too slow, but their contrary advice usually involves them selling you some "better way", so it's self-serving. It is worth remembering that if you choose to follow someone's investment recommendations, you have to follow *all* of their recommendations because there is no way to know in advance which ones will win and which will lose. They love to tout their achievements with a few examples of explosive gains, but how is their long-term track record when *all* their recommendations are taken into account? Add to this the hassle of watching for buy and sell indicators, entry and exit points, and money on the sidelines earning nothing while waiting for the optimum buying opportunity. The Newborn Nest Egg formula, on the other hand, can literally be set up in an hour, automated with monthly dollar cost averaging, and left alone for as long as you like.

Human nature tends to make us think that great performance requires great effort, great risk, or both. In investing, the opposite is true; remember the principle of being a contrarian. The *Newborn Nest Egg* formula offers very low risk for two key reasons: 1) with shares of just one ticker (**SPY**, **IVV**, or **VOO**) your portfolio is diversified across the 500 most important companies in America, and 2) you, and especially your kids, have long time-horizons in which to take advantage of sale prices whenever investor sentiment is negative by using dollar cost averaging. You also have lots of time to gain from those sale price opportunities when negative sentiment reverses. In this way it effectively covers both bases of the *buy low, sell high* principle automatically. Ultimately, it's the best way to build a wealth snowball that grows itself as your money is put to work for you; it's much more cost-efficient and time-efficient compared to investment-advisory, professionally managed investments, or any investment advice or portfolio management with ongoing fees.

The managers of these S&P 500 ETFs have a very easy job because there is no stock selection involved. That means no research, no analysis, no reports, no stock-picking, no high-priced experts of any kind, and no distribution channels with all the salaries, commissions, bonuses, fees, and perks that go along with selling other financial products such as mutual funds. In fact, an ETF can basically run itself automatically from a computer trading platform. All that is necessary in terms of human oversight is some fact-checking from time to time to be sure the holdings of the ETF continue to accurately mirror the S&P 500 Index. The company that curates the makeup of the S&P 500 is Standard & Poor's. Their role is to analyze and review which companies to include in their list, or index, to be sure it represents the 500 leading U.S. public companies. Changes are required once in a while as major companies go through mergers and acquisitions, market capitalization changes, financial distress, spin-offs, etc., but the changes are few and far between. For all these reasons, the management fees of an ETF are trivially low.

Historically the S&P 500 has been around since 1957, so that's 67 years at the time of this writing. But that's just the curated list, the actual companies comprising the original index were around a lot earlier than that. If you ask that crucial question about whether the

S&P 500 is going to survive and thrive for another 50 to 100 years, it would be hard to imagine a scenario where it wouldn't. Unless America itself is gone, there will be 500 most important companies trading on public stock exchanges that can be selected for this index. No single company or market sector you could invest in today is likely to have as certain a long-term future as the S&P 500.

The benefits of investing in just one single S&P 500 ETF are numerous. Each of the example ETFs is made up of the same 500 leading public companies in America, curated by a sterling, long-standing financial institution. Each ETF provides the same vast diversification across every major market sector. They include numerous multinational corporations, so they have exposure to international and emerging markets. They include miracle growth companies like Apple, Microsoft, Tesla, Amazon, Netflix, Alphabet, Meta, NVIDIA, Adobe, and SalesForce.com. They are not watered down by the inversely performing components of a balanced portfolio like bonds. They track an index that has had a long history of excellent performance. They are extremely efficient in terms of management fees. They incur no selling costs because they have no sales and marketing infrastructure. And they allow you to automatically reinvest dividends.

In other words, this one simple investment simultaneously meets all the criteria outlined in all the wealth-building techniques that have been presented throughout this book.

In summary, the S&P 500 is about the only type of investment that is virtually guaranteed to continue unaffected by management teams, technology advancements, competitive forces, or world economic events, for decades to come. It is therefore the only type of long-term investment you can truly set-and-forget, and expect to generate out-sized gains for generations.

With the standard disclaimer that past performance is not a guarantee of future returns, let's have a look at how each of the three example ETFs have performed:

- The oldest of them is **SPY**. It was formed by Standard & Poor's Depositary Receipts (SPDR) in 1957 in parallel with the inception of their S&P 500 Index itself.

- **IVV** is managed by BlackRock, which is the world's largest asset management company. Their assets under management (AUM) are approaching $10 trillion. Their S&P 500 ETF, ticker symbol **IVV**, was established in the year 2000.

- Vanguard is a large investment management company headquartered in Malvern, Pennsylvania, known for its focus on low-cost index funds and ETFs. It has a unique structure where the assets it manages, and the company itself, are owned by the fund shareholders. This is designed to strategically align the interests of the company with those of its clients. Vanguard's S&P 500 ETF, **VOO**, has an inception date of September 7, 2010.

The Compound Annual Growth Rate (CAGR) of the three sample ETFs, since the inception of each, has been as follows:

- SPDR (**SPY**): 10.5% CAGR since its inception in 1957

- BlackRock iShares Core (**IVV**): 9.66% CAGR since its inception in 2000

- Vanguard (**VOO**): 10.06% CAGR since its inception in 2010

The investment returns of each of these ETFs is greater than the CAGR of the S&P 500 Index itself over their respective timeframes because they include dividends and reinvestment of those dividends. For our purposes of making forecasts of future returns we will assume a 10% CAGR. Obviously, this is just an estimate but there are decades of evidence behind us showing that the average long-term performance of the S&P 500 has always been in this range. Over shorter terms the 10% rate will *not* be the expected performance, it will almost always be greater or lesser, but for investors with long-term outlooks (25 years or more), this is a very reasonable growth rate to use for planning.

16

What does it take then to create a million-dollar nest egg for a newborn child? You may have noticed a few subtly placed, and some conspicuous, hints throughout the book. They were meant to be an Easter egg trail leading to the answer, which is $16. Yup, that's $16 per month per $million! I gave you the entire page before this one to clear your head of all other information so that this can sink in. As you can see in the chart below, you could start with $0.00 when your child is born, invest $16 per month, and generate a million-dollar nest egg for their retirement, assuming a long-term CAGR of 10% for your chosen S&P 500 ETF.

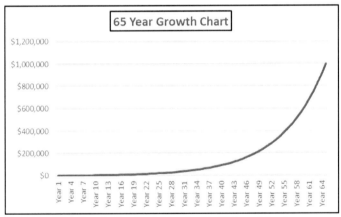

This Result Can be Achieved with $16 per Month

Note that these results can be achieved much more quickly and efficiently if you have a starting amount greater than zero dollars to invest. The chart above shows graphically how long it takes to get the value off the ground. But then, just like a real snowball, once it has some mass it starts growing exponentially faster. Look how much more quickly the second 1/2 million dollars is generated compared to the first half.

127

On the $16 growth trajectory, it should take about 58 years to reach the first $1/2 million, and then just 7 years to generate the second $1/2 million. That's why the saying is so true that your first million dollars is the hardest one to make, and therefore the most important.

The truly astounding part of this scenario is how much of each million dollars is earned by the investment returns as compared to the money your family contributes. Your contributions over the years are $16 per month, times 12 months per year, times 65 years. That's only $12,480 contributed *by* your family, and $987,520 earned *for* you, passively, by your relentlessly working money! That's a 7,900% return on investment!

If the revelation that just $16 per month can generate a million-dollar nest egg for your newborn didn't get your attention, hopefully this will. Look back at the sample family budget in Chapter 3. I said I would demonstrate how a million-dollar nest egg could be created with a family income of less than the average from two full-time workers. Notice that the remainder, the bottom line, of that sample budget, which is based on this very achievable level of family income and expenses, is $320 per month. What this means is that at $16 per million, you could choose to generate $10,000,000 nest eggs for each of two children (like Bill Gates ;). Do you need another blank page to collect your thoughts? Go ahead, read this paragraph again and look at the graph below. Yes, it actually shows that you can initiate not just a $1,000,000 nest egg, but a monumental $20,000,000 nest egg on an average family income. And your family's total cost for this twenty-million-dollar fortune is only $12,480 per million, spread over 65 years. This is the power of compounding wealth.

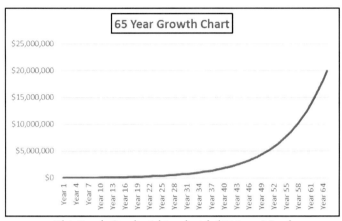

This Result Can be Achieved with $320 per Month

Also notice that by about year 34, the nest egg will have grown to a million dollars, and by year 48, to about $4 million. Any time after that the nest egg will be earning enough on a monthly basis that the recipients could potentially retire from earning income from other sources. Also, continuing to contribute $320 per month becomes much less important. That ongoing monthly contribution could readily be transferred to nest eggs for the next generation.

The following table can be used to determine approximately how much would need to be invested on a monthly basis to achieve your desired nest egg amount in your desired timespan, assuming a starting lump sum investment of $0.00 and a CAGR of 10%.

Investment Timespan (Desired Retirement Age minus Current Age)

Target Nest Egg Amount	65	60	55	50	45	40	35	30	25
$1 Mil	$ 16	$ 25	$ 41	$ 66	$ 106	$ 172	$ 280	$ 462	$ 771
$2 Mil	$ 32	$ 50	$ 81	$ 131	$ 211	$ 343	$ 560	$ 922	$ 1,541
$3 Mil	$ 47	$ 75	$ 121	$ 197	$ 317	$ 514	$ 840	$ 1,382	$ 2,311
$4 Mil	$ 62	$ 100	$ 162	$ 261	$ 422	$ 685	$ 1,120	$ 1,843	$ 3,082
$5 Mil	$ 78	$ 125	$ 202	$ 327	$ 527	$ 856	$ 1,400	$ 2,303	$ 3,852
$6 Mil	$ 93	$ 150	$ 242	$ 392	$ 633	$ 1,028	$ 1,680	$ 2,764	$ 4,622
$7 Mil	$ 109	$ 175	$ 282	$ 456	$ 738	$ 1,199	$ 1,960	$ 3,224	$ 5,393
$8 Mil	$ 124	$ 200	$ 323	$ 522	$ 843	$ 1,370	$ 2,240	$ 3,685	$ 6,163
$9 Mil	$ 140	$ 225	$ 363	$ 587	$ 949	$ 1,531	$ 2,520	$ 4,145	$ 6,933
$10 Mil	$ 155	$ 250	$ 403	$ 652	$ 1,055	$ 1,712	$ 2,800	$ 4,606	$ 7,704

But wait, there's more: similarly incredible results can be achieved even more quickly, and more efficiently, if you have a starting investment amount of more than zero dollars. Instead of $12,480 being paid by your family for every million dollars by your child's retirement age, it can be done for as low as a one-time investment of $2,050! That's about 600% more efficient.

The following table can be used to determine approximately how much would need to be invested as a one-time lump sum to achieve your target nest egg amount in your desired timespan, assuming no additional monthly investments and a CAGR of 10%.

Investment Timespan (Desired Retirement Age minus Current Age)

Target Nest Egg Amount	65	60	55	50	45	40	35	30	25
$1 Mil	$ 2,050	$ 3,300	$ 5,300	$ 8,600	$ 13,800	$ 22,100	$ 35,600	$ 57,400	$ 92,500
$2 Mil	$ 4,080	$ 6,570	$10,600	$17,040	$ 27,500	$ 44,200	$ 71,200	$114,700	$185,000
$3 Mil	$ 6,120	$ 9,860	$15,900	$25,560	$ 41,200	$ 66,300	$106,800	$172,000	$277,000
$4 Mil	$ 8,160	$13,140	$21,200	$34,100	$ 54,900	$ 88,400	$142,400	$229,300	$369,500
$5 Mil	$ 10,200	$16,430	$26,500	$42,600	$ 68,600	$110,500	$178,000	$286,600	$461,500
$6 Mil	$ 12,240	$19,710	$31,800	$51,150	$ 82,400	$132,600	$213,600	$343,900	$553,800
$7 Mil	$ 14,280	$22,990	$37,100	$60,000	$ 96,500	$154,700	$249,200	$401,200	$646,100
$8 Mil	$ 16,320	$26,280	$42,400	$68,200	$109,800	$176,800	$284,800	$458,500	$738,500
$9 Mil	$ 18,360	$29,560	$47,700	$76,700	$123,500	$198,900	$320,300	$515,800	$830,700
$10 Mil	$ 20,400	$32,850	$53,000	$85,200	$137,200	$221,000	$356,000	$573,100	$923,000

Note from this table the colossal power of getting your money working for you. A one-time investment of about $2,000 can earn your child a million dollars if left in a 10% CAGR investment for 65 years. You work to earn the initial $2,000, but putting that relatively small amount of money to work earns $998,000 more – passively. And from that point on it can earn about $100,000 per year. We have already seen how much more efficient up-front investments can be compared to monthly investments. On the other hand, lump sum investments are more difficult to come up with than the minimal monthly amounts, plus monthly investments take advantage of dollar cost averaging. Both strategies have their advantages so a combination of the two may be the ultimate prescription.

You can use the two tables above in combination to determine how to earn a retirement nest egg of multiple $millions in far less than 65 years (or visit www.NewbornNestEgg.com and use the calculators). For example, if you want your child to have a comfortable retirement nest egg of $4 million by the age of 55, you could achieve it by combining a one-time investment plus an ongoing monthly investment. Pick an initial lump sum that should generate $1 million in 55 years, then add the monthly commitment to earn an additional $3 million in the same timeframe. That would require about $5,300 upfront, plus $121 per month. That may present a bit of a challenge but is very workable on an average family income if it's a priority. If your incomes are above average, it should be no problem as long as you budget appropriately. Asking both sets of your kids' grandparents to help, especially with the one-time, upfront investment, might make it easier for you and very rewarding for them. Imagine explaining to them how they can give each new grandchild a retirement gift of a million dollars for just $1,000, matched by another $1,000 from the child's other set of grandparents. For all you know, they may choose to contribute enough for several $million, providing incredibly valuable lifelong safety nests for their grandchildren.

Clearly, the value of any investment portfolio will not go up linearly, in other words, it will not be a straight line up and to the right. The principle of a wealth snowball, or compounding, makes the growth charts look more exponential. But even that is just the anticipated *average* performance, not the *actual* performance expectation. It will no doubt be a somewhat random-looking series of ups and downs along an exponential path. Two factors within this strategy are linear, however: the time factor and the contribution factor. Let's take the simple example of building a nest egg on a 65-year timeline, and assume we're only using monthly contributions to achieve it. In other words, whatever size nest egg you are aiming for by your child's by retirement age (which may be much different from the age at which they are able to retire from having to work for their money), they will be one-quarter of the way there by age 16, halfway there by age 32, and so on. Their portfolio value may not be, but the investments of time and money will be. Here is what that timeline will look like in terms of dollar contributions:

If your kid(s) are not exactly newborn when you initiate this strategy, you will have to contribute more per $million or plan for a later retirement. Rather than clutter the next few pages with various examples, several calculator functions have been built into the accompanying website www.NewbornNestEgg.com. There you can experiment with various initial investment amounts, the ages of your children, monthly contributions, etc., and visualize the expected results. When you lay your golden nest egg (i.e., initiate your investments), please help other new parents by sharing your experience on social media and in an Amazon review, or wherever you found this book, or just lend them your copy of the book.

For those who want to become more informed investors, and wish to understand how well alternative strategies might perform compared to an S&P 500 ETF, Appendix A has been provided. I highly recommend you read it, but first read the upcoming chapter and follow its instructions to initiate the Newborn Nest Egg formula outlined above.

CHAPTER 7

PASS IT ON

Today a million bucks might seem like a lot to you, and it's definitely a good start. It is a lot better than not having a million dollars, that's for sure. And the truth is that many of your generation won't ever achieve it. Even the next generation that you are raising may never get there without a jump start in both a nest egg fund and the knowledge to grow it further. Many don't understand how simple it can be, or they prefer to try a bunch of different things in the hopes that one of them will eventually generate the big payoff sooner. Some will always prefer to blame anyone and anything else for their circumstances, lack of opportunity, and barriers to success. You, on the other hand, are now a *Newborn Nest Egg* investor with enough wisdom to know this straightforward formula, you have made the commitment to start using it today, and you will stick with it long-term. You know enough not to get sidetracked by every shiny object and better-sounding scheme that comes along. You know that work doesn't have to be hard if you work smart and do things you love. You also know that the smartest thing to do is not to work for your money forever, but to get your money working for you, and your kids, as soon as possible. Committing funds to the *Newborn Nest Egg* investment might not always be easy, especially at first if you plan to start with a significant lump sum, but before you know it your family will have foundational wealth, financial independence, and a pathway to generational wealth.

By now you are most likely aware that a one-million-dollar net worth will not exactly enable your kids to retire in luxury many years from now. You know that inflation will erode its buying power, but do you really know what a million dollars will be worth when your kids choose to retire? Of course not; nobody does. Should you give up like others do because financial independence seems out of reach, and money won't have as much value by the time they acquire it? It will have less than today's buying power, for sure, but it will still be significant. Whatever you do, don't assume that enough wealth for a nest egg is not worth pursuing. That's what people do who will never have even one million dollars in net worth, which statistically is most people. The math is undeniable, and I can confirm from experience, that the first million dollars is the hardest to acquire; which makes securing that first $million the most important.

Inflation is inevitable, and it will definitely eat into the buying power of whatever wealth you generate. But that's not unique to our time and place in history, nor to this wealth-creation strategy. Inflation is just a fact of life, and it makes the creation of wealth even more urgent. The future will undoubtedly cost more but the growth and earnings of the most important companies in America will increase right along with it, vastly outpacing inflation. The most dangerous financial position to be in is where you *don't* have gains being generated for you by the key engines that drive our economy.

Your Children's Safety Nest

Consider this hypothetical scenario. Let's say that you choose to invest $2,000 up front, and add $100 per month, from birth, for each of your children using the *Newborn Nest Egg* formula. That should provide each of them with a retirement nest egg of over $7.4 million by the age of 65. As each child becomes an adult and fully understands and takes ownership of the wealth-building strategy you put in place for them, they can start contributing their own money. If starting at age 20 they commit to growing their nest egg with an additional $300 monthly investment of their own, their combined safety nest would total approximately:

- $1.5 million by age 45

- $4 million by age 55

- $10 million by age 65

This would be in addition to any 401(k) plan they might invest in along with their employer, and any net worth they might accumulate via real estate investments such as a condo, a house, or a commercial property. It is also additional to the value of any business they may own by that point in time. These are all very achievable investment amounts, even with nominal incomes. This situation would allow your child to retire by age 55 with their portfolio earning about $400,000 per year. If they could live on half that amount, supplemented by 401(k), IRA, and/or other pension income, the other half would keep the portfolio growing to outpace inflation, and its increasing value would still be there to pass on to the next generation.

This 'safety nest', the synergy of a safety net and a nest egg, for your children yields a total that is far greater than the sum of its parts. Yes, it can generate enough capital to comfortably retire early and still provide generational wealth, and it can do so without significantly constraining the lifestyle of ordinary income earners. But it is so much more than that. Having this growing foundation of wealth all through a person's life opens a whole world of choices. They could choose a career that is very fulfilling to them, even if it doesn't pay very well, without worrying about their long-term financial security. If they want to pursue greater wealth, they can take some risks like investing in more volatile opportunities, as long as they are always unwavering in their safety nest commitment. They could also start a business, which might otherwise be devastating if it failed, but would be glorious if it succeeded. They could pursue more risky careers in the arts, like acting, comedy, music, painting, writing, social media influencer, etc. If they make it big in one of these ventures, great! If not, they always have the safety nest to fall back on. They can pursue their dreams and passions, whatever those turn out to be, and still pass on tremendous wealth and financial wisdom to the next generation. When people reach a position where they no longer need to work, they often find ways of making even more money because this situation provides both freedom and confidence. Such an environment can stimulate and inspire creativity, innovation, and invention, leading to monumental success.

Character and Integrity

A very intriguing thing happens when a person no longer thinks of cost as a major consideration in making decisions. For the majority of us, throughout our lives, we consider cost as one of the most critical factors in every decision we make, whether it involves purchase decisions or lifestyle choices; and that's the right thing to do until we're financially independent. We must consider financial limitations when it comes to grocery shopping, entertainment, travel, what we wear, vehicle purchases and operations, the home we live in, and everything else up to and including health care. But once we are set-for-life, and our money passively earns more than we spend, everything changes. This is when a person's true character and integrity come to light. What a person does with their life when money is no longer the limiting factor in their decision-making is very telling; it amplifies their character traits, both the strengths and the flaws.

When we're wealthy there are substantial benefits, both for our health and our demeanor, due to reduced stress and anxiety. No longer are we worrying about making ends meet, getting fired or laid off from a job, providing for our family, or the cost of unforeseen repairs or health issues. Instead of basking in the benefits of reduced financial pressure, however, some people over-indulge or behave selfishly and arrogantly when they reach this juncture. A mature person already knows the dangers of such behavior: overindulging in destructive lifestyle activities that deteriorate their health, blowing the money on pointless status symbols and ending up impoverished, damaging relationships with friends and family, or alienating anyone who is seen to be of lower income status.

Money won't solve everything; acquiring it is most definitely *not* the meaning of life. It's not even the real reason to generate wealth. The primary reason to pursue financial independence is so that your time and energy are available for more noble pursuits, and the most noble pursuit is to help others.

As Mother Teresa was often quoted as saying, "If you want to change the world, go home and love your family".

Love definitely starts at home, so start by loving your kids in a tangible way that enables them to do the same for others. The nest egg gifts you give them are not complete until your kids understand innately that giving is better than receiving. That way they will undoubtedly pass it on; sometimes called paying it forward.

Before gifting the nest egg to your kids it is important to ensure they are equipped to handle both the wealth and the responsibility. If you instill wealth wisdom while your kids are growing up, they will likely be ready to take over the duties of continued growth as they enter adulthood. The monthly amounts necessary to create generational wealth over the long term are so small that kids could start contributing to their own nest egg fund from their own income while they're in high school. With the right level of explanation, kids can actually begin to understand and contribute to their own nest egg from an even earlier age. Many children receive gifts of money from relatives and friends for birthdays, Christmas, graduation, holidays, etc. With the right encouragement, they could choose to contribute a portion of these funds to investments. This can instill a mindset of responsibility, self-reliance, delayed gratification, financial planning, and good judgment. If they mature enough through good parenting, high standards, and great expectations, they may be ready to completely take over their nest egg gift just as they start their careers. This would be the ideal scenario for you as parents because it conveys financial responsibility to your kids at a time when you could start to enjoy your own retirement.

If that transition is successful, the juggernaut you have unleashed is much more likely to evolve into generational wealth.

The mature wealthy person, who no longer needs to consider cost as the greatest factor in decision making, will have their true character revealed by how they live. They can become more generous, helping those who are less fortunate or were not given the same opportunities. They can give back to society out of gratitude for their parents, circumstances, country, and infrastructure that enabled them to generate wealth. They can volunteer in areas that can benefit greatly from their depth of knowledge and wisdom in whatever noble specialty they pursue in their career. They can also share their knowledge, teach their skills to others, and mentor those whose lives can be dramatically improved by learning valuable skills early in life. The quintessential proverb is true: "If you give a person a fish, you feed him for a day; if you teach him to fish you feed him for a lifetime".

If you studied the sample budget in some detail you will have noticed a line item for charitable donations. You will also have noticed that it is not in the Discretionary Spending category. Having a charitable attitude, evidenced by real charitable contributions, goes a long way towards *being* wealthy. It can be very tempting to cut out charitable donations as an easy way to increase the bottom line for wealth generation, but it is important to avoid that temptation. As mentioned in Chapter 1, money in itself is not the end goal, it is just the fuel that drives the engines of our lives, enabling us to accomplish more of what we consider important. Helping others is the more noble pursuit that gives our lives meaning. Yes, it starts at home, but it should not end there. It is another habit you must develop from the beginning, and impart to your children, in order to experience the lifestyle and mindset of an honest millionaire. If the habit of giving doesn't start early, it is unlikely to develop later in life, or when you have more wealth, because charity, like wealth itself, is a mindset. Our reasons to generate and manage wealth wisely should not simply be to indulge ourselves but to become better human beings. Our goal should be to make life less desperate for others, and to help them become more self-reliant like we are. Desperate people do desperate things. Don't let that be you or your family. Especially don't let it be those less fortunate who simply can't work or support themselves for whatever reason.

I will not recommend or endorse any specific charity but please do your research and donate to those that genuinely help the less fortunate, either domestically or internationally. Be sure the organization has very low administration costs so that the majority of what you give is passed through to the needy. Especially avoid charities whose only purpose is to raise awareness of the plight of something or other; those don't really help anybody. Consider the fact that you always give a gratuity for good service at a restaurant, and you do it because it's the appropriate way to show your appreciation. There is no need to give 20% to charity as you do to waiters but think of charitable donations as a similar indication of your gratitude. In this case it's gratitude to humanity; not for services rendered, but for the freedom you enjoy to pursue unlimited opportunities. Remember that charitable donations are tax-deductible, so they only cost you about one-half to two-thirds of what you donate. Government programs pay the reminder in the form of reducing your income taxes. So give more than your budgeted amount, knowing that your actual cost will be lower based on your income tax bracket.

Invite Competition

There is one more aspect of the *Newborn Nest Egg* formula that is the inverse of the get-rich-quick schemes. Most money-making programs work best when there is very little competition. The total market size for most products and services is limited, so any competition tends to dilute the revenues of all suppliers. Investing in an S&P 500 ETF has the opposite effect. The principles of supply and demand would make the value of each share go up as more participants make investments. And this is not an irrational or fictitiously elevated value. The real values, often referred to as the intrinsic values, of the component companies underlying the stock index generally go up *because* their share prices go up. A higher share price allows these companies to raise additional capital more easily, and at better valuations, thus giving them a less expensive way to put more funds to work in product development, marketing, sales, acquisitions, and economies of scale in manufacturing, distribution, etc. There is an insightful saying that states, "Nothing succeeds like success". This is true of public companies and of capitalist economies in general. Money used for profitable enterprise is the fuel that drives up the real value of companies and countries, enriching all participants. In capitalist economies the old saying is true: "A rising tide lifts all boats." It means that more investors buying stocks raises the price of all stocks. Rising stock prices make companies more successful, and successful companies boost the economy as a whole, enriching everyone. For instance, companies like Apple, Microsoft, and Amazon have each created many thousands of millionaires among their early employees, executives, and long-term shareholders. This is what's known as a virtuous cycle – the opposite of a vicious or destructive cycle.

What does this mean for you? It means that the more people you can get to join you in following the *Newborn Nest Egg* formula, the better it will work for all participants. Feel free to lend your copy of this book to your friends and extended family, and to post about it on social media. This might sound like a thinly veiled promotion of my book but believe me, any possible benefit I might receive is not the point. I am already financially independent and in a phase of my life where I get much more fulfillment by giving back. My true motivation is to improve your well-being, that of your family, those with whom you share this book, and those you support through charity.

If you now agree with me that there is a right way to generate wealth for every stage of life, and the *Newborn Nest Egg* formula is the right strategy for new parents, please let me know your thoughts and feedback by rating this book with comments on Amazon, or wherever you found it. I am always particularly interested in how far into multimillion-aire territory my readers plan to take the *Newborn Nest Egg* formula. More information and tools such as investment growth calculators and budgeting templates can be found at www.NewbornNestEgg. com. There you can also provide direct feedback and even ask specific questions.

If you know people with older kids; those just starting their careers, or about to, you may wish to recommend the next book in the *Fast Wealth* series. It teaches the fastest and most assured formula from start-of-career to set-for-life. It can be found at www.FastWealth.com.

Get a Cup of Coffee with Your Spouse

After you and your spouse have both read this book, put it down but don't put it away. Go get yourselves each a cup of coffee, and while you sip them, look back and find the 10 steps of the *Newborn Nest Egg* formula in Chapter 16. Also, grab your computer or smartphone and use it to implement the first nine steps of the formula. Before your coffees get cold you can have the formula working for your family.

I performed a test on a subject who is a new father to see how long it would take him to implement the formula once he had read this book and come to an agreement with his wife on a monthly investment amount. I gave him no further coaching or recommendations than what he had read in this book; he had exactly the same information you now have. It took him twenty minutes to research and select an online brokerage platform, create an account, and choose one of the three recommended S&P 500 ETFs. It took him a further 40 minutes to link his new brokerage account to all his bank accounts, including retirement accounts, and automate the whole process. He set up an automatic transfer of a fixed sum of money from his bank account into his brokerage account on the first day of every month. He then set his brokerage account to automatically buy that same dollar amount worth of S&P 500 ETF shares on the second day of every month, and selected the option to reinvest dividends. Then he finished his coffee.

A young mother of three with no previous investing experience was my next test subject. I had asked her to review this book prior to publishing, and as she did so, she immediately decided to implement the formula. She was skeptical that it could be done as quickly and easily as the book claimed, but was pleasantly surprised and confirmed to me that everything was set up and automated in about an hour.

Don't forget about step 10 of the *Newborn Nest Egg* formula. There is no great hurry but sometime between now and the next time you file your annual income tax return you should get tax advice from an accountant regarding the most efficient setup of 401(k) plans and IRAs (or whatever tax deferral and tax shelter retirement programs are available in your country) for your family's circumstances. Any amount of money you have already put to work by that time can easily be transferred into different accounts at a later date if there are tax advantages to doing so. The important thing is to get a systematic program in place now so that your money is being put to work immediately, and every month from now on you will always be the richest you have ever been.

Your kids will never be younger than they are today!

APPENDIX A

PROOF IN THE PUDDING

Why make Investing so Simple?

A simple S&P 500 ETF investment satisfies all the wealth creation criteria that have been presented throughout this book. If you have read it carefully and implemented the formula you are now a competent investor, knowing a lot about how to keep investing simple, passive, automated, and stress-free. You also know a lot about how *not* to invest; especially how to void the expensive services of the wealth management industry, and this is critical!

There are numerous intricate investment strategies that can often sound ingenious in their complexity. These were intentionally left out of this book because they are unlikely to serve you well unless you have a hefty portfolio and vast experience, or you use the services of expensive professionals to do the heavy lifting for you. Even then, the results are frequently less impressive and less predictable than just being a long-term shareholder of the key drivers of our economy. Have a look at the following summary of how each tenet of the *Newborn Nest Egg* (*NNE*) formula is satisfied by its singular-focused, quick, simple, safe, stress-free, powerful, investment strategy:

No ongoing fees	You are now an NNE investor – no further training or paid services are required.
Start early	NNE recommends starting at birth, or as young as possible.
Remain resolute	NNE requires an unwavering, career-long, commitment.
Doesn't hamper other lifestyle ambitions	NNE works even if investing so little on a monthly basis that it is barely noticed.
Most valuable resource: Time	NNE is the ideal formula for long-term investment – generates enormous wealth for those with a long time-horizon/runway.
Budgeting leads to bounty	The budgeting exercise empowers users to make the tradeoffs necessary for NNE investing.
The snowball effect	The long time-horizon of NNE is ideal for massive compounding
Instead of working for money, get money working for you	The NNE formula gets your money to earn hundreds of times as much as you put into investments.
Buy low	Lump-sum investing far in advance, and dollar cost averaging, both ensure buying low.
Sell high	The ideal holding period is forever – never fire your most productive employees: your money earning passive income streams from investment.
One-hour formula	NNE can be initiated and automated in just 1 hour, just once in a lifetime.
Set-and-Forget	No adjustments are required after setup, unless you wish to increase investment amounts.
Everyone can do it	Not just anyone but everyone. In fact, the more participants the better it works for all.
Generate passive income	The one-hour set-and-forget strategy means all returns on investment are essentially passive income.
No salary cap	Working for money has its limits; investments have no upper limit.
Wealth from an ordinary income	Average American incomes (or equivalent in other countries) can generate multimillion-dollar nest eggs.
Generational wealth	Recipients of the NNE can retire, live off a portion of their investment income, and create nest eggs for the next generation.
Lifelong safety nest	Knowing there is foundational wealth being generated provides numerous lifestyle, confidence, and social benefits.
A dollar saved is two dollars earned	Cost-cutting and investing the proceeds provides adequate investment capital without requiring a pay raise, promotion, or side hustle – although all of those can boost the results.
Wealth depends on how much you keep	Many who earn a lot spend more than they make. You can be richer than them by following the NNE formula.
Avoid bad debt	Paying interest on depreciating assets is money working against you instead of for you.
Good debt can add to nest egg investing	Investment in your primary residence or revenue-generating real estate can add to the NNE effect by leveraging your down payment with a mortgage.
Opportunity cost	Eliminating costs like new cars, or additional cars, and investing the difference, can generate enough for a lavish nest egg.
Avoid depreciating assets	Depreciating assets rob you of funds that could otherwise be earning returns for you.
CAGR	The NNE formula benefits from the CAGR of the most important economic engines of our economy.
Don't lose money	Wide diversification and investment in the fundamental drivers of the economy ensure that money won't be lost in the long term.
Net worth	The NNE formula certainly increases financial net worth, but its principles also enhance generosity and integrity in the recipients by instilling maturity, confidence, and wisdom.

Very broad diversification	The NNE formula ensures that even very small initial investments are diversified across the entire broader market.
Avoid balanced portfolio	Balanced portfolios may be valuable for short-term or draw-down investing but are a formula for mediocrity in long-term investing.
Avoid financial planners and wealth managers	All industry participants must earn their collectively massive incomes from the portfolios of its clients. NNE avoids it all by being self-directed.
Dollar cost averaging	Small to medium monthly investments ensure that share accumulation takes place through all market downturns and sentiment anomalies.
Massive returns on investment	Due to its long time-horizon, the NNE formula generates massive ROI up to tens of thousands of percent.
Enduring investment	The NNE formula specifies investment in infrastructure that's sure to survive and thrive for as long as any financial entity on earth.
Avoid market watching	The set-and-forget strategy relieves NNE participants from the worry of watching market performance.
Always the richest you've ever been	The automated NNE formula ensures that each month you are the richest you've ever been, either in terms of portfolio balance, shares held, or both.
Know when to hold 'em	The vast diversity and intrinsic value of NNE investment ensures that shares can always be held instead of sold at a loss.
Automated from home	With today's online services, all systems required to set up, automate, and administer the NNE formula can be done quickly and easily from home.
Take advantage of 401(k)s and IRAs	The investments of the NNE can be incorporated into corporate and government retirement investment policies and programs
Tax advantages	NNE can take advantage of government tax deduction and tax deferral programs.
Most important public companies trading on American exchanges	The NNE formula specifies investment in the greatest drivers of our economy, providing better returns than most professionally managed portfolios due to avoiding management fees.
Honest wealth	Wealth brings out the true character and integrity of its possessor by eliminating cost as the key factor in decision-making.
Pass it on	<ul><li>Pass on financial nest eggs to your children</li><li>Impart wealth wisdom as children mature</li><li>Transition wealth-building process as children begin careers</li><li>Share the NNE program with other new parents</li><li>Give to charity and help those in need</li><li>Provide feedback encouraging others creating safety nests</li></ul>

How do Other Investments Perform?

There will always be very enticing financial advice or investment schemes that come along and sound so much better than a boring old S&P 500 ETF. Over short time periods, some of them might prove to be somewhat better. But again, that's not the whole story. New products, companies, industries, and investment strategies come along all the time, and the results often look so exciting. Investment advisors will present the past results of some of their best stock picks and show that you could have made gains like x, y, and z; often presenting a few examples that made hundreds of percent gains in a short time. But when you look at the long-term performance of *all* their stock picks combined, it's not so great after all. Over long timespans, especially decades, nobody seems to consistently or significantly beat the broad market, yet it takes *so* much time, effort, and risk, to try.

The issue is primarily one of timing. If you happen to get into a new investment opportunity at the right time, and then get out at the right time also, you could make out very well. You will have successfully bought low and sold high. Good for you! But timing the market is almost never a repeatable occurrence. Some guru will claim to have discovered a secret or unknown strategy to time the stock markets reliably, but don't believe it. Getting a few things right does not mean it can be repeated forever. As soon as some new opportunity or strategy appears to be working, everybody piles into it, and it becomes the new normal. This results in a lot of investors looking for the next big thing, and the cycle repeats itself. Bouncing in and out of these waves of popular investments opens up a lot of chances for failure. All it takes is to get in or out at the wrong time once or twice and your portfolio returns are poor, or even negative. The chances of getting both in and out of short-lived investment trends reliably and repeatedly are extremely slim. Sooner or later, you will miss an entry or exit point and generate losses that will devastate your portfolio, require unrealistic gains just to recover your losses, and lead to desperation investing, a.k.a. gambling. Don't lose money!

I am not saying that the S&P 500 provides the greatest possible returns in all circumstances. What I am saying is that you have the opportunity to set a strategy that is virtually guaranteed to work, automate the process so it just happens every month with no effort, and then focus on other things till you retire and turn over the newborn nest eggs to your kids. To do better than the 500 leading companies in America over the long term is very unusual, unlikely, and more risky. If you were to spend your entire time focusing on market research, following the best strategists and advisors, and jumping on the latest trends, you *might* do a bit better, but the evidence doesn't show many successful cases, especially over the span of decades.

With the *Newborn Nest Egg* formula, you still get the benefits of all the successful new trends because the biggest and best of these new companies are the ones being added to the S&P 500 Index over the years, while displacing companies that have run their course. This also avoids investing in the "promising" start-up companies that are sometimes a flash-in-the-pan, and can be losing investments when they fail to live up to the hype (look up the history of WeWork as an example). Your time will probably be much better spent earning additional income, and boosting your ETF snowball with it, than actively and intensively changing investments all the time. If you or your kids, as they become adults, have the time, interest, training, experience, and money to focus on active investing, great; give it a try. But first set and forget your *Newborn Nest Egg* strategy so that you always have a virtually guaranteed long-term success formula working for you, and for your kids. This will be your financial foundation; what we've called a safety nest.

Let's compare our strategy to other alternatives that may very well be presented to you as recommendations. The typical sales pitch will go something like this: "Why would you invest in the whole S&P 500 when you could just invest in the best-of-the-best companies from within that group? Don't you know that the 80-20 rule applies to the S&P 500 as well – where 20% of the stocks make 80% of the gains? Let our experts pick the top 20% of companies in every market cycle and your portfolio will vastly outperform the S&P 500!" It sounds so logical and so easy, so let's see how well these alternative investments have actually done over the long haul.

First of all, the S&P 500 Index is not just a flat list with equal representation from each of the 500 member companies. The index is weighted by market capitalization, which means that the more valuable companies automatically have a greater impact on the index's performance. The 80-20 rule is therefore essentially baked in. Secondly, it is difficult to find any managed funds whatsoever that have produced 50-year track records, yet you may need at least a 50-year runway from today to grow a nest egg big enough that your kids can retire from day-to-day work. Providers of managed funds are referred to as Asset Management Companies (AMCs). A critical factor to keep in mind is that all of them involve some form of investment selection, typically stock picking. This means that their performance relies heavily on the talent and skill of the management team, plus some degree of luck. These teams change over time, so the performance is also bound to change. Also, a team or strategy that performs well in one market cycle may do very poorly when conditions change.

Here are examples of some of the best alternative long-term investments and how they have performed. Note that all of them are based on services that provide either professional advice on how to invest, or they provide professional management of clients' capital using their own discretion. That means fees must be charged to their clients to pay for all the expenses.

- **Vanguard Group:** Vanguard is known for its low-cost index funds. Over the past few decades, the CAGR for some of their broad-market index funds, such as the Vanguard Total Stock Market Index Fund (**VTSAX**), has been approximately 8-10%, depending on exact buy and sell timing. This is no better than their own VOO S&P 500 ETF but it has been one of the best alternatives over the long term.

- **Dimensional Fund Advisors (DFA):** DFA is an investment management firm known for its evidence-based, factor-focused approach to investing. They encourage a long-term perspective and discourage market timing or attempts to predict short-term market movements. Historically, DFA has focused on serving institutional clients, such as pension funds, endowments, and financial advisors. However, their funds are also available to individual investors through financial advisors. Performance varies across their different funds and strategies, and specific entry and exit timing, but their approach has produced CAGRs ranging from 8-12% over the past several decades.

- **T. Rowe Price:** Founded in 1937, T. Rowe Price Group, Inc. is a global investment management firm that provides a wide range of financial services, including mutual funds, separate accounts, retirement planning, and investment advisory services. They are known for their active management approach, emphasizing fundamental research, long-term investing, and a focus on the intrinsic value of securities. They have a team-based investment approach where portfolio managers and analysts collaborate in making investment decisions. Total AUM is currently about $1.45 trillion. Performance varies across their different funds but CAGRs have been in the range of 8-12% over certain time frames, depending as always on entry and exit timing.

- **Berkshire Hathaway (Warren Buffett and Charlie Munger):** Berkshire has underperformed the S&P 500 in three of the past five years. Investing in this company is interesting, and different from any other single stock. A single share of the original stock (ticker symbol **BRK-A**) will cost over $600,000 at the time of this writing so it's definitely not for everybody. But there are class B shares (**BRK-B**) that are fractional equivalents; currently trading for about $400 each. A share of **BRK-A** or **BRK-B** actually gets the shareholder some ownership of a bunch of companies, because Berkshire Hathaway is a holding company, so it is pretty well diversified with its own holdings. Shareholders also get one of the best financial management teams in the world without having to pay all the fees associated with AMCs. Berkshire Hathaway has never paid a dividend and reportedly never will. Nevertheless, over the past 40 years, they have delivered an impressive CAGR in the range of 15-20% depending on exact buy and sell timing. But Charlie Munger, vice chairman, died in Nov 2023, about a month shy of his 100th birthday. Warren himself is almost 94 years old at the time of this writing. Once he is gone, who knows what the next 50+ years will bring? He has been saying for quite a few years already that it is much more difficult to grow at the same percentage rates as they used to, now that their size is so massive. Their current market cap is nearing $900 billion, $167.6 billion of which was in cash as per the 2023 year-end report. According to Buffett, there are very few investment opportunities large enough for them to invest in for any outstanding gains, and the few that exist have been endlessly picked over by himself and other large investment fund managers. He concludes his 2023 annual letter to shareholders by saying, "All in all, we have no possibility of eye-popping performance."

That's why the greatest investor in history has consistently recommended that most people invest in the entire market via a low-cost index fund such as an S&P 500 ETF. "They'll earn the average market return – which after fees will outperform the vast majority of professional money managers." Buffett also frequently warns investors to avoid the financial advisory and wealth management industry.

Despite all the infrastructure, experts, effort, energy, strategy, and machinations used by AMCs, none of them consistently or significantly beats the S&P 500 over the long haul. There is a fundamental reason for this, and it can be demonstrated with simple math. The fact is that not everyone can be above average. If you were to ask anyone whether they are above average, the vast majority will say that they are. The same goes for companies. Their PR departments have only one job; to ensure that the public recognizes them as one of the best. But the mathematical principle called the law of averages is indisputable. The common joke is, "Be careful out there, 50% of all doctors graduated in the bottom half of their class". The same holds true for financial advisors and asset management companies. By the law of averages, in any given timeframe, about half will beat the market and the other half will do worse; that's just how average performance is calculated. The sum of all funds invested in the stock market IS the market, no matter who makes the investment decisions. The performance of the broad market is therefore the cumulative performance of all investors, including experts, professionals, institutions, and individuals. The above examples of long-term track records of the best-performing Asset Management Companies in the industry prove that the math can't be very wrong for very long. Some might beat the broad market for a while but over the long haul, they all tend to be average, except that the fees they charge make their returns below average for their clients.

The fees associated with buying, selling, and administering a portfolio of managed funds or mutual funds can have a significant impact on an individual investor's returns. These fees are separate from the reported performance of the mutual funds or AMC-managed funds, and always reduce the overall return realized by the investor. So don't be fooled when the reported performance of these funds sometimes look pretty good. Take into account the fees they charge when you calculate what *your* real return would have been.

The two main types of fees associated with mutual funds and AMC-managed funds are sales charges (loads) and management fees (expense ratios), which include ongoing administrative and other operating costs.

1. **Sales Charges (Loads):**

   a. **Front-End Load (Sales Charge):** This fee is charged at the time of purchase, and it is a percentage of the total investment amount. For example, if you invest $1,000 in a fund with a 5% front-end load, $950 will be used to purchase shares, or units, of the fund, while $50 will go toward the sales charge. But this puts you 5% in the hole before you even get started, so your first 5.5% of gains will just bring you back to break even. Except they won't quite, because of the other fees described below.

   b. **Back-End Load (Deferred Sales Charge):** This fee is charged when you sell your fund units or shares, and it is also a percentage of the redemption value. The fee may decrease over time and eventually reach zero if you hold the fund for a long enough period. Sounds good, right? Well, there is still no free lunch. The reason a mutual fund or managed fund can forego their back-end load after enough time is that along the way they will have charged you management fees. If you do pay a back-end load it could be a greater amount than a front-end load because presumably there will have been growth along the way, and now your fees are based on a percentage of that larger sum. Don't forget, they are charging ongoing management fees on the value of your entire fund holdings. This includes your initial investment plus any gains they may make in your portfolio.

2. **Management Fees (Expense Ratios):** This is an annual fee expressed as a percentage of the fund's average net assets. It covers the costs of managing the fund, including administrative expenses, advisory fees, and other operational costs. The expense ratio is deducted from the fund's assets, and it directly affects the investor's returns.

In addition to sales charges and expense ratios, there may be other fees associated with mutual funds, such as:

- **Transaction Fees:** Some funds charge fees for specific transactions, such as buying or selling shares or fund units.

- **Redemption Fees:** These are fees imposed when you sell fund shares or units, primarily to discourage short-term trading.

Spend a few minutes studying the performance data of the twenty professionally managed funds listed in the chart below. These funds are managed by some of the best-known AMCs in the industry. You will notice a few incredible gains over short timeframes but by the time you get to the 10-year column (highlighted), the longer-term CAGR of *all* of them has been abysmal. Notice that all of them have an expense ratio as well, so an investor's actual returns would have been even worse. Some of them charge a front-end fee or a back-end fee in addition. These are not necessarily the best-performing funds on the market, but they are examples of real-world funds that are professionally managed and have long-term track records, so they are a fair comparison to the *Newborn Nest Egg* formula. Have a look at

PNRZX for example (highlighted). Can you imagine paying management fees for ten years and experiencing performance like this? Investors paid them fees (EXPENSE RATIO) of 0.92% of their entire portfolio every year, and over a ten-year timeframe, they lost 11.99% of the portfolio value, on average, every year! In other words, after ten years investors were left with only about 28% of their original investment. Yet incredibly this fund still contains $0.53 Billion worth of FUND ASSETS under management.

*Fund Assets are listed in $Billions. All returns, expense ratios and loads are listed in %

NAME	TICKER SYMBOL	FUND ASSETS	1YR. RETURNS	3YR. GACR	5YR. CAGR	10 YR. CAGR	EXPENSE RATIO	FRONT LOAD	BACK LOAD
VANGUARD GLOBAL CAPITAL CYCLES INVESTOR	VGPMX	$1.08	12.07	-5.47	5.44	-5.87	0.38		
FIDELITY SERIES COMMODITY STRATEGY	FCSSX	$5.84	-2.92	-3.02	-4.26	-9.87	0.01		
PGIM JENNISON NATURAL RESOURCES Z	PNRZX	$0.53	0.22	-4.09	-1.22	-11.99	0.92		
INVESCO OPP STEELPATH MLP INCOME A	MLPDX	$1.74	-28.73	-12.47	-9.12	-2.93	1.39	5.50	
INVESCO OPP STEELPATH MLP ALPHA Y	MLPOX	$0.62	-30.82	-15.29	-12.09	-2.92	1.34		
ALPS/CORECOMMODITY MANAGEMENT COMPLETE COMMODITY STRATEGY I	JCRIX	$0.50	0.19	-1.72	-0.60	-2.80	1.14		2.0
FIDELITY SELECT ENERGY	FSENX	$0.69	-30.84	-14.91	-9.33	-2.77	0.81		
USAA PRECIOUS METALS AND MINERALS	USAGX	$0.83	38.22	20.98	22.15	-2.53	1.27		
FRANKLIN GOLD AND PRECIOUS METALS A	FKRCX	$1.34	46.28	20.03	20.78	-2.19	0.98		
VANGUARD ENERGY INDEX ADMIRAL	VENAX	$2.72	-31.25	-14.45	-8.75	-1.99	0.10		
FIDELITY SELECT GOLD	FSAGX	$2.76	36.13	16.37	21.18	-1.96	0.79		
SPROTT GOLD EQUITY INVESTOR	SGDLX	$1.33	34.16	14.84	18.16	-1.44	1.47		2.0
AMERICAN CENTURY GLOBAL GOLD INVESTOR	BGEIX	$0.88	31.25	20.01	14.00	-1.39	0.68		
INVESCO OPP STEELPATH MLP SELECT 40 Y	MLPTX	$1.79	-29.92	-13.63	-0-7	-1.30	0.89		
INVESCO OPPENHEIMER GOLD & SPECIAL MINERAL A	OPGSX	$2.36	45.41	21.82	25.46	-1.13	1.16	5.50	
VANGUARD ENERGY ADMIRAL	VGELX	$4.55	-22.2	-9.26	-3.40	-0.95	0.24		
VANECK INTERNATIONAL INVESTORS GOLD A	INIVX	$1.15	43.85	20.42	24.01	-0.47	1.45	5.75	
AB ALL MARKET REAL RETURN 1	AMTOX	$1.00	0.28	0.57	2.47	0.16	1.11	4.25	
JANUS HENDERSON OVERSEAS D	JNOSX	$1.20	16.88	4.16	5.42	0.19	0.79		
INVESCO INCOME A	AGOVX	$0.59	-9.57	-1.77	-0.50	0.66	1.01		

The Data Above is from Morningstar Direct

You will recall the example of Apple (**APPL**) that was presented in Chapter 5. It has historically produced incredible growth rates over most timeframes, but even Apple's growth chart isn't always up and to the right. Over the past 12 months, its CAGR has "only" been 11.27%. This, and other massive companies like it, will increasingly have a harder time growing at the same percentage rates as they have in the past. If you ask the fundamental question of whether Apple will still be a dominant consumer electronics company in 50 years, you can't confidently say yes. So far, they have been trendsetters but what if they miss the boat on artificial intelligence, blockchain technologies, quantum computing, virtual reality, or some other key technology that hasn't even been dreamed of yet? A new company that starts up in the garage of someone's parent's house, like Apple did in 1976, could be the one to displace them as top dog in the consumer technology world in the next twenty or thirty years. By itself, **APPL** would be a risky bet for a long-term investment strategy today. As part of a portfolio of 500 leading companies it's great because it will likely contribute a lot of the dividends that can be reinvested. If it fails to perform decades from now it will be removed from the S&P 500 Index and a new superstar company will be added.

> **The point is that for a virtually guaranteed way to ensure your nest egg grows at a rapidly compounding rate for decades, it's very hard to beat all the benefits of the S&P 500. And an ETF is the most cost-efficient way to invest in that broad market index. Make the commitment, set it and forget it, and then move on to the more noble pursuits of your life and career.**

Financial planners and wealth managers typically generate long-term returns of about 6% CAGR, net of fees. My personal experience with their services resulted in even less than that but let's give them the benefit of the doubt and say they could do 7% on average over the long term. Nevertheless, look at a comparison of the typical professionally managed returns vs. the typical S&P 500 returns. This 3% reduction in annualized returns results in about 1/4 of the net result in the long run. Stated another way, you could generate four times as much wealth in long-term investments by avoiding the services of paid advisors and their balanced-portfolio recommendations.

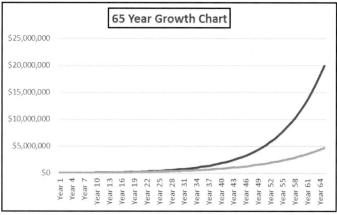

Long-Term Comparison of 7% CARG to 10% CAGR

To be fair, over short timeframes the professionally managed returns are often less volatile, and therefore could be considered less risky. If you have less than a twenty-five-year time horizon for investing, perhaps for your own nest egg funds as distinct from those for your children, you might consider a professionally managed portfolio. If you get to a stage of life where you require a steady income from your investments, and are considering a drawdown of your portfolio, it might be wise to seek the help of a wealth management professional. But if you have the typical runway available as new parents to build your own nest egg, and *Newborn Nest Eggs* for your children, which ROI in the chart above would you prefer? Remember, if you do it right and have built up a large enough portfolio, neither you nor your children will ever have to draw down your investments to a smaller portfolio. You can simply live on something like half the annual gains, and let the rest continue to grow for generations to come.

About the Author

R. Fast is the developer of the *Newborn Nest Egg* formula. He and his wife have taught this material since 2005 to young couples preparing for marriage and families, and they have witnessed impressive, consistent results by those who implement it.

Mr. Fast learned financial principles through his career in corporate management of technology companies where he held positions of P&L responsibility including CTO, COO, and President. He also founded two tech start-ups in which he was CEO. One of them he took public through an IPO, and the other was sold to a Venture Capital group. It was not these endeavors, however, that made him financially independent; it was implementing the principles presented in this book.

Mr. Fast is currently Chairman of the Finance Committee of a charitable organization with several thousand members and a multimillion-dollar annual budget. He is also Chairman of another foundation that holds real estate assets in the range of $100 million in value for use in non-profit operations.

Besides investing, Mr. Fast's current endeavors include travel, consulting, teaching classes and seminars, volunteering, spending time with family and friends, and writing books.

ALSO BY
R. Fast & Fast Wealth

Please visit the websites associated with this book. There you will find free supplemental content and articles as well as several free calculators, sample budget templates, and more. You can also leave comments and ask questions.

At FastWealth.com you will find subsequent books in the *FAST Wealth* series as they are published.

www.NewbornNestEgg.com

www.FastWealth.com